Grenades as Lullabies

By Manja Lazarevic Rodriguez

DEDICATION

There is something marvelous that happens when one liberates his or her voice. When their truth, regardless of previous teachings, society, opinions of others, is spoken and lived by them entirely. I have awakened; and yes, this book was part of my awakening. Thus, with all my heart, I dedicate this book to everyone who has been a part of my journey. My dear parents, my amazing family, my soulmate husband, my incredible kids, my mentors, my friends, past and present, my clients, and many more. I'm eternally grateful. However, the primary dedication goes to my sunshine, to my teacher, to my eternal love, my daughter Layla. Thank you for being the Earth and the sky for mom. I love you to the moon and back. Bear Paw. HEART!!!

PREFACE

When your life is about to change forever, sometimes it's time to look back. I remember sitting, pregnant and hormonal, and telling my story to a stranger who leaned in with rapt attention. I had never thought my life was that different or intriguing (does anybody ever think that?). It was impossible to deny, however, that this person – like many before them – was intrigued, even inspired. That motivated me too. I rubbed my swollen belly and decided to write about my history. If for no better reason than my children would have something they could hold on to after I pass on. I want to tell the world what happened to me, everything that was on my chest filled my heart, and shaped my soul. This memoir of the happenings is based solely on an innocent child's perspective and opinions. 'Grenades as Lullabies' is a personal story of war and innocence.

So here it is, for all who need it. My story. Thank you for listening.

Chapter One

I never realized how beautiful the passages and forests of Mount Jahorina were, nor how much they would save my life one day. Mount Jahorina is a lovely Olympic mountain in the heart of Bosnia. The greenery and evergreen trees that surround the entire mountain is a sight out of magazines. Every tree, every rock is entirely coated with moist and glistening moss. Gorgeous hills roll to its peak of 6,568 feet. One beautiful day, in the late spring of 1991, my family and I were on our regular outing in the meadows in the mountains near Sarajevo.

While perched upon a big, smooth rock, my eyes drank in the outskirts of the forest where we camped. The massive pines towered above me. I was just a tiny dot on nature's surface here, and yet at one with the comforting sense of harmony in this place. The sun sneaked through the occasional cloud. A light breeze with a subtle smell of pine needles caressed my face. I closed my eyes and took a deep inhale that filled my entire being. I drank in the majestic nature and sat in wonder at how beautiful and peaceful my country was.

I enjoyed being out there, especially with my family and friends. We'd spread out a volleyball net, make boundary lines out of tape, and laugh through hard-fought tournaments. My uncle, Nuno, was excellent, but my dad, Bruno, was not far behind. They played hard. Dad never passed up the opportunity to show off his athletic skills. These outings were the perfect place. He was a professional soccer player in his earlier years, and his body showed it. His hair is brownish red, and his nose has a slight bump, which I was lucky to inherit as well.

We played soccer, went mushroom picking, and marveled at how the smell of the charcoal grill made the whole atmosphere complete. My mother, Alma, was in charge of feeding everybody – ever the nurturer. She's a tiny, petite blonde beauty. I always thought she looked like a movie star, with a matching outfit, even here in the forest. Her heart was still in the right place.

Our camping vacations always went by so quickly. Sundays were the worst because they meant leaving my cousins and friends and going back to school. Even though my school was fun, I would rather be running across those fields, communing with nature. Finding that harmony, I still yearned for so much. My weeks were pretty typical: school, homework, play outside with friends and repeat. I did well in school, it always seemed to come easy, but it never fully satisfied me. I enjoyed the art and creative classes the most, but I was still happiest daydreaming. I never felt in the right place, living in Sarajevo, even though I couldn't fault the life my wealthy parents had given me. I had everything. I was an only child, and we enjoyed our experience. Somehow, however, I always felt the drive to do something unique, somewhere different, being in a different world.

We traveled a great deal. My family was big on vacation. By the time I was nine, I had visited ten different countries. There were day trips to Milan to go shopping for the latest Italian trends. Mom had to have the latest furs and shoes, and I enjoyed the change in the atmosphere. We took the ferry across the Adriatic Sea with our car, staring at the reflection of our coast in the mesmerizing sea. The smell of the seaweed and fresh sea air was a remedy for anything. The sea was absolute heaven. The water was always crystal clear, even in the deep. The sight of our coast from afar was magical, tall mountains behind the rocky beach at sunset. A postcard picture that every tourist sent back home. The coast of Italy was another magical place - beaches and greenery mixed with marine life. It felt like another world. Those travels built the foundation for the open-minded and cultured person I would become.

Our last vacation to Turkey in the summer of 1991 as a family was the most memorable. I saw fascinating places and ate terrific food. Only in Turkey would a restaurant prepare eggplant forty different ways for an appetizer. These kinds of delights were the reason I started to become a little too chubby.

The variety of everything was incredible. Turkey offered the sight of short shrubbery and tall evergreen trees juxtaposed beautifully amongst the tall palms. A unique feature of the Kusadasi town where we vacationed was the natural hot springs. Natural craters over spilling with warm water that shimmered with white sparkles covered the mountain, reflecting the light for miles. Hot smoke billowed into the air as we sat in the hot springs and rejuvenated in the water's deep remedy. Even with such wonders around me, what I remember most was how happy we were. How much fun my family had. My mom was always dolled up and smiling. Dad was a true gentleman, content, and – most importantly of all – always holding my hand.

If it was not a trip to another county, there was always a road trip to somewhere, often to the community mountain cottage. I liked it there the best. The cabin was beautiful. It was built on the flat top of a hill, in the forest of Bjelasnica, right next to Jahorina. Sarajevo, my lovely town, was in the valley they surrounded. Driving an hour in any direction would reach the majestic mountain of your choice. Bjelasnica was best known for hiking and camping. Just getting to the cottage was an adventure in itself. We would drive up into the forest, then through a cut-out rock tunnel in a cliff on the smallest two-way road, you have ever seen. Beyond the rock tunnel, was a shoulder with two to three parking spots. From there you could look up a gorgeous hill of pure grass and flowers everywhere. Then, right at the top, you could make out our dreamy cottage. We left our cars there and hiked for ten minutes. The hill was even steeper than it looked. Going up and down a few times would put an end to a day, but it was always worth it.

We usually invited my aunt, on my dad's side, and her family to join us at the cottage. There was always something very mysterious about that place. I think it was the intimidating forest that sat right behind it. Just the thought of going near it gave me chills. Often, we would hear the bears at night coming out of the forest, following the scent of food. My heart would always pound so hard that I could never sleep, but the bears never harmed us inside the cabin, they were used to people. The wood cabin was charming, with a fireplace and antique school furniture and a kitchen. It was an actual camping site. We all slept in wooden bunk beds. It was great to be together. We never forgot how essential it was for us to keep our family together and spend quality time. We used to gather inside and listen to the sounds of the guitar my cousin played. That was my beautiful lullaby at the cabin. Little did I know that soon I would become used to a far different lullaby – one of violence and war.

As good a time as we had, the reality of life was always there. My parents worked a lot. Mom was a lead architect and damage assessor for the whole northern part of the country, gone for days at a time. Dad ran the parts department for a big military company and worked long hours. When they traveled at the same time, I would stay with my grandpa, Ratko, my dad's father. He was medium-sized, bald but with a very fit body for an older man. He had the most beautiful blue eyes and a smile that made anyone feel infinitely better, even in the worst of circumstances. He raised Dad after his wife died of breast cancer when Dad was only three. I always had such respect for him.

Ratko was a true gentleman, but a lonely one. I guess that's why we got along. I missed Mom and Dad while they were away, and he loved to have somebody with him as much as I did. He was ready for board games, cards, or puzzles. As a former mountaineer, he was enthusiastic and full of life and energy. I learned a lot from that amazing man. Grandpa Ratko taught me about our history and different cultures through exciting and scary stories from WWII and facts about the past. I would sit there and listen, sometimes in tears. He also shared with me the stories of our country. I found it surprising how culturally mixed Yugoslavia was, all due to a long history of empires like the Roman or the Turkish Ottoman Empires overtaking the country.

Our land had always been feuded over until our leader, Tito, took over. Ratko loved Tito – like everybody in the country did – because he gave us peace, brotherhood, and good living. Some history books depict him as a dictator but, to us, he was a kind leader. He was tough on foreign influence and made our military strong, nobody would bother us, even here in the center of Europe. Tito demanded taxes, but he also provided a safe place, free education, free healthcare, and the freedom to have a lucrative private business. My aunts and uncles were few of many private business owners that thrived under his reign. Tito kept the peace, and he united all religions, not only to co-exist, but also to celebrate each other in love and unity. Bosnia was the only place where you could hear Orthodox, Catholic, and Muslim church bells calling at the same time. Grandpa Ratko taught me all that and much more.

The most ironic thing about Grandpa was that his last name – Lazarevic – came from Orthodox Serbian descent, but, he was baptized in a Roman Catholic church like my dad. Lazarevic was considered to be Serbian by some standards. "Political idiocy and propaganda," my grandpa would say. I never paid too much attention to that, but I learned as much from my grandpa about the orthodox beliefs as I did the Catholic Bible. I found both very interesting. Knowing about religions was helpful when it came time to build my belief system. We all lived together and observed the religious holidays of many faiths: we celebrated Christmas, orthodox Christmas, Muslim Ramadan, and Jewish Holidays – all the while it never mattered to me whose last name was from which descent. I do admit that as a child, though, all I often cared about were the presents and great food on every occasion. The condos where Grandpa Ratko lived were indeed a mix of all religions and cultures that summed up Sarajevo and the whole country – unity, love, and celebration for all.

One of my favorite things was to celebrate Ramadan with Mom's side of the family, which was so big! I was always learning of new cousins I had almost every visit. There were a lot of kids my age, and that made it so much more fun. My Grandma Emina and Grandpa Huso lived in the old part of Sarajevo, far away from our suburban home or the downtown area, where Ratko lived. Mom's youngest brother, Muris, and his family lived with them in a big, antique, white Mediterranean house that was hundreds of years old. It boasted a beautiful, Turkish architecture style with a huge yard that had a Turkish fountain and a lovely brown gate.

There were houses like that all over the old city, where Turkish and Arabic architecture was very prominent. I loved visiting every vibrant part of the old town, drinking in the variety of churches and mosques that cut a gorgeous skyline against the lovely sunsets. I greatly admired the beauty of the ancient city, as well as the technological swirl where it was allowing itself to transform to look more like the cities of the modern world. Towers of brick and gleaming skyscrapers added to the pure new culture of nature co-existing amidst the busy cityscape.

My mother's passion for architecture was alive and well in me. Strolling through the historic city of Sarajevo was purely magical. We would walk down the strips of ancient streets, stepping carefully over cobblestones that were thousands of years old. We shopped in busy street markets that sold beautifully handcrafted coffee cups, souvenirs, blankets, and Turkish crafts. I listened to the song of the Hodjas, calling people to prayer from the tower of the white-arched mosques. They all had towers capped by a golden reflective top, each topped with the

Islamic half-moon and star. Hodjas are Muslim leaders, like priests, that call out from the top of the mosques to remind Muslims to pray five times a day. Somehow, the Hodja's voice magically blended in harmony with the dinging of the bells from the churches right beside. The sounds would travel and follow us as we slid through the narrow, medieval passes of the old buildings.

Those passages were so mysterious, so exciting. Most of them made of brick. Some blended with the streets, while others had many different colors framing heavy wooden doors with high thresholds. Each entry had its unique design as if everyone was telling the story of their past, their history. Balconies, filled with white gardenias, gave a sense of safety and calm, even in the mysterious passages. It was all so beautiful.

The tunnel effect always caused the most refreshing winds to blow there, cooling and caressing your face. It also brought with it the smell of freshly baked loaves of bread and cevapi, a town delicacy made of small beef sausages grilled on firewood to perfection, then served with pita bread and sour cream and onion. The soft-grilled pita bread complimented the tender and tasty sausages in a way that made me my senses tingle; my mouth salivated just at the thought of them. The town was amazing, and it lived together in harmony with nature and its people.

Up in the hills was my Grandma Emina's beautiful white house, in a neighborhood that was a joy for families. It was mainly a Muslim area, according to the sometimes-weird political formulas of last name recognition. However, my Serbian/Catholic father and his family lived so nicely and peacefully with Mom's Muslim side. All the neighbors knew each other, took each other food and visited daily.

Grandma Emina deserved all the incredible attention she got because she was the most beautiful person I have ever met in my life. She was small with blue eyes. I barely saw her lovely black hair because she always had it covered. This woman was beautiful in her way, with the most gentle soul. She helped everyone, no matter who they were, taking children in when they did not have a home and even avoiding stepping on ants. She had regard for every single life on Earth. Emina genuinely believed in the power of prayer and being a righteous person. She taught me everything.

For Emina, where there was a will, there was a way. There was nothing too hard or too demanding. Emina and Grandpa Huso accepted my dad into their family as their son, even if he was from a different religion. To them, it was love that mattered most. Huso was a kind man who would caress my face and tell me how precious I was. Though he sadly died of a stroke when I was only six, I much remember his warm, round face and soul-touching smile.

Since his loss, Grandma Emina was very lonely. I didn't like seeing her like that, so I spent every minute I could with her. I enjoyed listening to her stories about her life and well-off family and being in her presence. She had the most fantastic outlook on life. The Turkish influence her family had on her life and how it led her to where she ended up. She was short of a princess descent and had been under tremendous pressure to marry into the right family, but refused it all and decided to go her way and marry Huso, the love of her life. Emina also worked, kept her life together, and remained the rock of the family. She had fantastic independence and endurance to make everything she dreamed of come true. She always remained so gentle, sweet, humble, and giving. I admired that about her and wanted her to teach me how to achieve that.

Emina and my aunt and uncle taught me a lot about Islam as well. I learned the Quran and all of its intriguing stories. I owed her and my uncle for a deep understanding of what Islam preaches. Like all the other religions, it only calls us to be good people and follow the rules of prayer. I only remember the good and positive attributes of those teachings. The most interesting were the stories of the Quran, which I had the chance to compare to the Bible. My uncle encouraged me to believe but always told me that it was up to me to decide what I thought and who I wanted to be. All ideas were blessed, as long as I was a righteous person.

My grandma was just happy for me to spend time with her and listen. Every time we visited, she kissed my forehead and told me that I would be something special. She would always be there for me. Her intense blue eyes left a warm feeling in my heart, making me feel safe. During those moments, I deeply knew that she – one way or another – would always be there for me. I spent a lot of time there in the summer, in between the traveling sessions we took. I cherished and loved every minute. My family was great, my city was beautiful, my parents were awesome, and I just had a lovely, normal childhood for those short-lived years.

That time of beauty and unity, however, eventually came to a terrible end.

Chapter Two

The summer of 1991 in Sarajevo was as hot and beautiful as any other but, before we knew it, it was already early fall. Everyone was getting ready for a new season. Classes were about to start, but my parents were busy with preparations for a significant change in our lives. Mom had finally gotten the dream townhouse she had been working toward for a while. We needed to move in just a couple of months. Our new home was in one of the latest state-of-the-art neighborhoods, right by the Sarajevo airport, which was moving to another part of the city. In its place, they were going to build a vast recreational park with fields, courts, and swimming pools. It was going to be kid heaven.

They were building new schools in the area too, with modern buildings and technology. Mom always knew how to get the best deals and the most prominent things. She was an excellent businesswoman, and I admired her drive. I was very excited about the move. We all were. Why wouldn't we be? I mean, a bigger house, bigger yard, and a more beautiful neighborhood. I was finally going to get a room big enough for a complete working desk with shelves that covered the entire wall. Sure, I would also have to find new neighborhood friends, but I didn't worry much about that. I had always been very social and usually managed to make new friends and strike up conversations with just about anyone – even ninety-year-old people! I got more and more excited as the move approached, but the only thing that gave me pause was that we were going to be a lot further away from our family.

As we were preparing to move, I stayed a lot with Grandpa Ratko, because I was still going to my old school that was a lot closer to him. The days were ordinary enough, but I noticed something different about him. He looked a lot more withdrawn, sadder than ever. I would ask him if he was okay, and he would reply, "Ay, honey bunny. It's just me being an old fart, that's all." He wasn't acting like himself at all, so I pried further. Eventually, he admitted that our moving worried him, "I guess I'm... scared that I'm going to die alone." My little jaw dropped at this dismal, dark thought. I hugged him in my arms and comforted him, telling him that we would always be there for him, that he was not alone. He knew I spoke the truth, but it still made him sad to think that he was going to see us a lot less. We were going to have to get used to the idea that we were going to spend far less time together.

I did all I could to calm his worry, but, unfortunately, both of us knew that he was right. The new school had an afterschool program for me and, by the look of my parent's plans, he was not going to be my babysitter anymore. It was breaking his heart because I was all that he had that was close to him. His eyes teared up as he told me that he loved me very much and then repeated his dark worry that he did not want to die alone. He didn't want to *live* alone either, and I was the one that had always been there. I was too young to understand his pain, and all I could do was tell him that we would visit all the time and that he shouldn't worry. I teared up as I told him how much I loved him and promised that he would not die alone.

He never liked seeing me cry so, right away, he did whatever he could to make me smile. We ended up laughing together. He would make a silly face, and it made me feel better. It made him feel better too. That was important to me at the moment, but little did I know that he remained sorrowful. Grandpa Ratko was heartbroken by the move, and my parents did not mention the change in him at all. It was like they failed even to notice.

He was heartbroken by what was happening in Yugoslavia as well. Grandpa dedicated a lot of his time to the TV news and reading the paper and books. One day, as the move was approaching, he dropped his paper and explained to me that something terrible was happening. There was fighting and political disagreements in northern Yugoslavia. The war was coming our way, and it did not look good at all. Ratko compared those times to how WWII had started – with the army fighting in Slovenia for land. I did not understand, but his face said it all. He knew struggle and disagreement, all the figures being elected to run the parties, and all the troubles with the economy pointed to one thing: *a bloody war*. The news that day had shaken him in a way that I had never seen. It deeply worried me, but he went on to insist that everything would be okay, and my parents would take care of me. I calmed down a little, but his anxious face never entirely went away.

That night, I asked Dad about Grandpa's worries. He explained that Ratko had gone through a lot in WWII and that his old age was making him worry about little quarrels that would never come close to us. He reassured me that things were well and that the struggles were far away. I believed my dad. He was my hero and always had the best arguments and ways to persuade me to feel better. He honestly had a gift for that. He made me understand things in a new way by dissecting it and puzzling it all back together. That made me understand why so many people loved and respected him, why he knew so many, who would do anything for him. Of course, being nine, I soon forgot any worries about the quarrels and continued my life as it unfolded. I spent as much time as I could with Grandpa until it was time for us to move into our new house. I remember the day we moved very clearly. I hugged Grandpa so tight and told him that I would always be there for him. That everything would be fine. I would visit all the time and that I loved him very much. His loving hug back was just as beautiful and as powerful. That was the last hug we would ever have during times of peace.

Our new house was terrific. The view from the living room looked straight out onto the airport that was about a mile away or so. A big road and a lot of yard and greenery surrounded the buildings behind the airport. In the distance, you could see the beautiful mountains that surrounded Sarajevo. That view is unforgettable. The mountains were our protectors, a safe and secure wall that also provided beauty and serenity. The yard behind the house was perfect for play. There was also a park with a bunch of courts and swings. My room was everything I expected, with a wall-size shelf and a new bed. Due to her architectural instincts, my mom decorated it most tastefully. Everything was fresh, with beautiful furniture imported from Milano.

It was time to find new friends in this unique neighborhood. I went with my mom to meet our new neighbors and, hopefully, find new friends my age. Our next-door neighbor was a nice lady named Senka. She was a single mom, a widow, that had two children – Dino, an older son of eighteen, and Daniel, who was ten. Senka was so welcoming. The typical Muslim woman that would give us the shirt off of her back if we had needed it. She always fed us so well, giving me cookies, juice, and freshly squeezed berry juice. She was quick with a hug, especially for me. I always felt that she and I were close because she had always wanted a girl, and there I was – that cute little chubby girl that was nice and well-liked and got along with her so well.

Daniel was shy around me at the beginning, but soon, we became good buddies. I had a small crush on Dino, mostly because he was older but also because he was cute and tall, with dark hair and eyes and a charming smile. That was what got my heart pumping the most, his smile. I knew that I was dreaming about the crush ever being mutual, but it was fun to have those butterflies in my stomach. Daniel and I got along really well. We played outside a lot. He was my best friend at that time and was always on my team. He protected me from the other kids when we had our differences, but, in general, we all played together nicely and got along very well. Our favorite game was hide and seek. My friends could never find me in the neighborhood because I was always a step ahead of them, knowing where they would look, and when I had to change my spot. Eventually, they would give up, and I'd get all the points.

Being chubby, I was often the target of fat jokes from the kids, but they quickly learned to respect me because of my hiding skills. Daniel was proud of that, and always told me "not to mind any of those ugly idiots." He said the boys that made fun of me probably just liked me and didn't know how to act about it so that they would say mean stuff. The comments did hurt and sometimes sent me home in tears. I told my mom and dad about the nasty jokes and kids being cruel, but my dad was so awesome in calming me down. He said that, once I showed them who I really was, they all would want to be like me, "What matters most is that you are beautiful inside. Don't worry about what anyone else says, not even us." Those were powerful words that became a pinnacle of my ideology moving through life.

I clung to what my father and Daniel had said to help me feel better. I never let the jabs of others slow me down. Pretty soon, there was never a game, hangout, or birthday that did not include me, the chubby girl. Daniel and I came to be inseparable. I think this also had to do with the fact that our families were very close. We would spend a lot of beautiful, neighborly meals together. I used to stay at their house from time to time when my parents were away, and we formed a good bond. Daniel was like a brother to me. He was shorter than me and was skinny with a small face, blondish hair, and dark eyes. Our relationship wasn't about attraction. He was my best friend. We went to school together, and he kept protecting me, but I learned how to show my teeth as well. In return for his back-up, I always helped him with homework. I spent a lot of time with him, and I learned about his family and how he lost his dad to cancer. He didn't remember much about his father but still missed him. To help him, his brother served as a mentor and father figure. I also told him that I would always be there for him and that everything would be okay because my dad suffered the same thing with the loss of his mother. I assured Daniel that everything would work out and that he would grow up to be as unique as my dad. I would tell him all the time, "You are awesome, Daniel. You will see. You will be a hero one day." I told him that he was my best friend and he would always be great to me.

I also made friends with a timid Jewish girl named Jana. She was in most of my classes and was very smart. I learned a lot from her about Judaism, Hanukkah, and the meals they ate. She even introduced me to delicious, challah bread. She had long, straight hair down her back. She hung out with Daniel and me, but her parents did not let her play outside as much as we did. She told me that her dad was very protective of her "because of the kind of work he did," but she never could explain to me what that was. Regardless, I was glad to have a girlfriend, somebody to talk to about girl stuff. The new move went smooth for me, and I was happy that I was adapting so quickly. My parents were happy too. They made friends with most of the neighbors, so it felt like we were all getting along, and the neighborhood was safe.

We also still maintained our routine life and outings with our family, visiting my grandparents and cousins from both Mom's and Dad's sides. I always went with Mom to visit Grandma Emina. Mom felt obligated to bring her food and presents, and I loved going to see her too. I loved her so much. She always brightened my day. I do wish we all could have lived together so I could have been closer to all of them.

More than anything, however, I loved going to see Ratko. I felt terrible for not being with him more, no matter how much we tried to see him. He was so happy to see me every time. We had the best time together, but I could tell he was never entirely content. It seemed that something was bothering him. He was not entirely himself. I kept asking him what was wrong, but he said that it was just old age, that he was just fine. Right after moments of melancholy, he would instantly change his mood, and we would spend time laughing and playing games. His smile and his big hugs were the best.

All the days seemed to pass by quite the same: school was great, friends were wonderful, my family was outstanding. We traveled every chance we had and spent time having dinners and enjoying the holidays. I would say it was a pretty standard, and somewhat spoiled, life I led.

Then came December of 1991, and all I could think of was my birthday party on the 20th. Mom had prepared a big party. I was so excited. It was a cold day, but beautiful clouds surrounded the mountains and spread toward the city. Then, right at twilight, it started to snow. We always got our first winter snow on my birthday, so it was not a surprise. The snowflakes were mesmerizing, and they stuck fast to the ground and the cars. It was lovely how pretty everything looked, covered in snow. It made me feel that much more special on my 10th birthday. The only problem was that Dad was going to be the chauffeur for all the kids, transporting them back and forth. It wasn't comfortable driving in the heavy snow, but Dad was the greatest. So was Mom. They both made my party so great. Everybody showed up: all of my friends from the neighborhood and school, as well as my cousins. Jana begged to help with all of my presents. Daniel was there at the beginning and staying until I fell asleep from all the dancing and eating. He gave me a loving kiss on the cheek and told me that I would always be his best friend. I remember that day, that birthday, more than any other of my childhood. It was one of the best days of my life and one of my favorite memories of our life in Sarajevo.

The winter was as beautiful as always but very cold. The mountains in the distance looked magical to a young girl like me, all covered with snow. The heater in our new house warmed it just right. There was something different about this winter, however. It was cold in a way that no heater could soothe. My parents and I were barely going out. We hardly ever went to visit anyone, rarely venturing outside the routine of work and home. We went skiing only twice that winter. Just the year before, we had gone every weekend as a family. Now we just sat in silence – as a family too.

It took courage to ask my parents, "Is everything okay? Why are things different?" I already had an idea that it was because of the economic strife in our country. Mom couldn't answer. Instead, she held me tight, kissed my forehead, and scoured the news religiously. The stations reported that there was change looming throughout our country, and violence too. Our government was in turmoil. There were not enough resources. She was holding me more in those days, as she listened, learned, and worried. It made her want to be closer to me. She never let me out of her sight.

Dad would do his best to explain, simplifying with phrases like, "Things are not looking good." He worried that the government was falling apart. It was no longer safe outside. "My princess, the elections are not going well. We don't have Tito to save us. It's chaos out there, so we have to be careful and see what happens. We need to stick close to each other. It's not safe."

My heart sank. The mountains were looking less magical. The clouds that came over them seemed to hover around my head and choke the air from my lungs. With an exacting voice, I asked, "What do you mean? *Not safe.*" He told me of the numerous shootings and barricades set up across the city. That food transportation was scarce. His face grew pale. I was petrified, and my mind immediately raced to the thought of our family. I felt the temperature rising – that cozy heater now burned me like a furnace – and I started sweating as I pleaded, "What about Grandpa Ratko? He is old and alone. And the others? Were they in a bad place? Do they have enough food?"

I panicked as he hugged me. I was so worried. In my heart, I knew things were wrong, but the worst part was that I could tell this was only the beginning. I remembered everything Grandpa Ratko warned me about how wars start. I asked father, shaking and crying if this had anything to do with army troops in Slovenia, the northern part of our country. He nodded, but embraced me and told me not to worry, "Everything will be fine. Nothing bad will happen. Our army will protect us." He said they were arranging to bring Ratko to live with us for now. I kept spouting questions like a mad person, "What about food and school?" He whispered that we must continue to live normally, but with caution. That everything would get better. I cried on his shoulder, pleading, "Please get my grandpa here. Please."

Chapter Three

By the end of February, everything had grown even colder. I continued going to school, seeking comfort in my best friend, Daniel. He was always my protector; my everything away from my parents. He was growing taller and beginning to fill out, becoming a man – and I felt even safer around him. Though our parents always dropped us off and picked us up, I was still worried. I talked to Daniel a lot about the country's struggles. He said that things were getting worse, "Different groups are forming. Serbian fanatics are gaining power in the police force and the army. They're terrorizing other religions, like the Muslims and Croats." Daniel seemed as frightened as I was, "The government isn't going to help anyone. Serbs are abusing their power, and my brother is now obligated to the army. He will probably go very soon." His eyes were wet with tears. I hugged him but did not know what to say. His voice cracked, "He and my mom don't know if he can trust a Serbian-led army. He might join the TO." My eyes widened at the mention of this TO army, a privately held army, made of Muslims and Croats that fought against the corrupt Serbian army. I was stunned. All of us had always lived so peacefully together – Croats, Muslims, Jews, and Serbians – but now we were at each other's throats, all because of the Serbian army following the commands they were getting from their leaders in Serbia.

I thought of my family and what this meant for them. What they <u>were</u>. "My dad... he is Serbian. Has he done something wrong?" Daniel shook his head, trying to assure me, "Of course not. Not people like him. I'm talking about the crazy ones. " It was Serbian leaders from Serbia and corrupt politicians that wanted to conquer the Bosnian land. Tito was gone, and all parties wanted to "ethnically cleanse" our land for their occupation. The Serbs got to the resources first and had the upper hand to do just that. I was so scared: *How would the innocent be able to defend themselves?* I saw no light at the end of the tunnel, only worried faces. Dark skies covered the mountains, and the smell of trouble, uncertainty, and insanity.

That day, I also found out that Jana had disappeared. Her entire family was gone, as though they had been wiped off the face of the earth. I searched everywhere for her. Nobody knew where she had gone. They abandoned their house. I knew she would never leave, not like that. Daniel said that it must have been because her dad knew something. My heart sank.

He told me most of the Jewish families had left the neighborhood as well. His mom Senka worked in the grounds keeping and had witnessed them leaving for good, "They must know something we don't. Maybe Jana's dad warned them to go as well." Confused, I wondered *why they didn't warn us as well?* I put my head down as Daniel held me and walked me toward the front of the school. My mother picked me up and saw I was sad. She ran to me. I told her about Jana's family, and she held me and kissed me and told me that she was sure Jana would call. That maybe she had just moved somewhere. I could tell, however, that she didn't believe that either.

My parents did not say much; they just stared into the quiet night. They were going to pick up Grandpa in a few days and bring him here. They talked about leaving as well. They had sworn that things weren't going to get worse here, but they were — every day. We were running low on food, and there was hardly any to buy in the supermarkets. However, we stocked up on food as much as we could. Mom cried while my dad told her quietly that he would save us. I went to bed, trying to fight my anxiety, sorrow, and worry, and to find sleep somehow. Once I did, however, it was only to be awoken for one of the worst days of my life.

My panicked mother shook me, "Honey, get up! Baby get dressed!" That morning, the trouble got closer – so close it was right in front of our faces. Dumpsters were burning in our neighborhood, and groups of protesters going up and down our street with guns. They had blocked all traffic. The police were powerless. My face dropped, and I grew pale. I quickly packed a few clothes, my passport, and a few tiny, silly girlish treasures into my little school bag. I also grabbed my little stuffed rabbit with me. Anything that could remind me of how things used to be – to tell me of joy and happiness and my past routine life – wherever this new, awful reality was going to take us.

We stayed where we were, for the time being anyway. That was the first day I stopped going to school. On the first day, my parents did not leave for work. We, and our entire neighborhood, just stuck to the TV, stayed away from the windows, and tried to find out from neighbors what was going on. Daniel and Senka came over to follow the news. Mom did not want to let us watch, but we could hear that fanatic groups were blockading the neighborhood. Everyone was in danger. The government ordered us all to stay in our homes and proclaimed a mandatory curfew. I can remember having a weird feeling of excitement mixed in with my anxiety and fear. I was a child, so my emotions couldn't begin to process all of the danger looming.

My parents talked to all of our family members. In some parts of town, like the old city, there didn't seem to be any trouble at all. My uncle said people were still outside and working just fine. I finally got to talk to Ratko, and he sounded okay as well. I told him that I loved him and that we would come to get him soon. Dad smiled at me, but he told Ratko that we needed to wait a little while to see if our part of town would calm down first. We locked ourselves in our house day and night, following the news. Daniel and I stayed together with Senka, Dino, and my parents.

We children tried to play while the adults discussed the dire situation, in hushed tones. I asked, "Is this temporary? Or is it forever? I'm scared." Daniel just shrugged his shoulders; he had no way to bring me comfort. I was still adrift in that mix of fear and excitement. It was a terrifying situation, but something new and different was happening. We did not have to go to school, and my parents were with me. Bizarrely, it was kind of like a vacation. I later found out that this naïve optimism was just a defense mechanism. My young brain was working against my fear, fighting for survival. That night was long, but eventually, I grew sleepy. I finally snuggled up on Mom's lap with my bunny and fell asleep on the couch.

The next morning, I stayed right there. I felt rested, but quickly remembered the danger wasn't a dream. My parents were right next to me. I had not slept in my bed. They both looked exhausted, and I knew they had spent the whole night following the news. That day, I watched the news with them. It was interesting what I saw, which always depended on what channel Mom followed.

One TV station, apparently run by a predominantly Muslim population, was reporting that a Serb extremist group was causing all of the trouble and that no Muslims or Croats were safe out there. Another broadcast, played on the Serbian station, blamed the "Balije" – a demeaning term for Muslims. They claimed that it was the Muslim extremist groups that were terrorizing parts of the city. I could not believe that each side was blaming the other in this way, and I finally asked, "So who is responsible for all this?" Mom told me that the news was trying to do what was called "brainwashing" or "propaganda." She told me that there are good and bad people, but it was not about whether they were Muslim or Serb or Croat. It was the first time I heard of this word – "propaganda" – but I would quickly learn that it could cause chaos. My mother explained that they could tell that the group terrorizing our neighborhood were Serbs by their flags and the comments they were making. They were Serbian extremists, not like my dad and his family. I was so confused and needed to know more, "What Is a Serb, anyways?" I remembered all of the teachings I had from before, but this new reality seemed to cry out in the face of it all. Mom just responded, "There is no difference between all of us, honey. We all are human." I came to realize one thing; that our nation was getting segregated according to religious backgrounds, because of all the extremist sides. The innocent, in the middle, no matter what religion, they belonged to were suffering the most.

That day dragged on and felt like weeks. Every day after felt that way for so long. There I was, the best hide and seeker in the neighborhood, forced to hide in an awful new way. We were cowering in our house, listening to gunshots and violent outbreaks nearby. The airplanes no longer landed as often, and everything seemed to be disrupted and dying. Once in a while, we would lose our electricity and pray that it would come back, and be thankful when it did. We felt like trapped rats, not knowing what was happening, not appropriately informed, and with no help seeming to come from anywhere – not from the police or even the army. Mom took inventory of our food, and she was distraught. We did not have much at all. We would have to be careful to spread it out, but it became irrefutable: we had to go out there to find some food.

Dad agreed to go with neighbors to look for help, food, and weapons to protect ourselves. Our neighbor from a few houses down, Vedad, went with him. He had a small, blonde, blue-eyed, four-year-old boy named Luka. Against everyone's will, Dino insisted he go as well. He said, if he could not join the army, Dino would do anything he could "to fight these pigs." I guess it was the eighteen-year-old testosterone talking. My mom was worried about letting Dad go, but we needed food desperately and had no choice but to find out what was happening and what our next steps would be.

We were growing to understand that we were in the worst part of town. Nobody could go in or out, so we left Ratko at his house. I was terrified to let Dad go out there. My hands curled into fists, and I was sweating profusely as he went to the door. I told him we should call someone for help, but he just kissed me and said, "Don't worry. We will not go far, and I'll be back soon." That day brimmed with anxiety. Mom and I were on our feet the entire time. Senka was praying the rosary and, at some point or another, all the woman joined in.

When dawn came, the men were still not back. There was no way to reach them, and we had heard gunshots all through the night. All of us were panicking. I just stood there, unable to process my emotions. Somehow, my heart knew he was all right, but it was scary to listen to gunshots and wonder where they were. *Were they killing somebody out there?* My mind pondered the purpose of all of this.

Suddenly, we heard a commotion from outside! We were terrified but, thank goodness, it was the men coming back, running to seek shelter. I was so happy to see my dad. They were all right and *loaded* with stuff. They carried full bags of food, flour, sugar, canned stuff, and bread. I also noticed that every one of them packed a big shotgun. That was weird and scary. They looked so huge and bulky. I hadn't yet learned how evil guns indeed were.

Once they had safely stowed the guns, I hugged my dad as if I would never let go. Eventually, both my mom and I settled down for another long night of strategy and following the situation. I stayed up as long as my body let me, listening to as much as I could catch of the adults talking. The men had gotten a lot of the food from the Muslim TO. The markets were abandoned, and there was no food anywhere. They had given them guns once they made a deal to fight with them against the extremists in my neighborhood. It was oddly funny, all three men were from different religions, but now they were all a part of TO, "The Muslim Army," fighting to survive and help each other. That's when I realized TO, in this case, was more than just a Muslim army. It was a "People's Army," fighting for their lives and their families, no matter what narrative Serbian TV tried to spin.

I knew that there were innocents on each side, both being terrorized by each other. The hatred spread fast, but here the TO were just neighbors and people sticking together as a human race. Regardless, the situation was looking grim. We had to fill containers with water and gather as many candles and batteries as we could. The TO was trying to help out, but we spent our days staying put and just surviving. My parents called for help on occasion, but the response was always that they were dealing with the situation the best they could. We talked to our family, and they were all worried. The situation was starting to worsen everywhere else as well. The whole city was disintegrating, becoming separated. Who was to blame varied, depending on which news source you believed. Neighborhoods that were predominantly one religion were uniting against others, and a vicious cycle was continuing.

Nevertheless, the other neighborhoods were still a lot better off than ours. I guess that's because the airport area was the first to get affected. In other areas, people could go outside and still buy food and be safer than we were. Even then, I was apprehensive about Grandpa Ratko. The only things that kept me calm were the facts that his neighbors often visited him, he had food, and he was in a safer part of the city, as was the rest of my family. They were all okay but feeling the onset of an actual turmoil. This was precisely how Grandpa Ratko had described how wars start, and it was unfolding very rapidly.

Chapter Four

Time continued passing so slowly. The days started merging. All we did was stay on the lookout, little by little protecting our house windows and doors, putting mattresses on the windows and creating a safe zone. I spent time with Daniel, playing board games, and talking. I told him that we were going to get out of this and go to school again, but he was furious. He wanted to fight too, just like his brother. We spoke about escaping and going somewhere. Those days and weeks were a blur. All we were doing was surviving, living this abnormal life, just wondering what would happen. We couldn't go anywhere, even if we tried. Before we knew it, the end of March came and, thank God, the weather warmed a little. That was the only good thing happening. The only entertainment was listening to gunshots and trying to recognize which one was which. By that time, I knew that my dad's gun was a Kalashnikov rifle, and I knew the sound of it too well. The days went by, and we were like prisoners in our houses. I thought that was bad until I woke up on March 23rd, which is when my world crumbled away and became even worse.

It was early in the morning when the phone rang at the house. Dad answered, and by the sound of his voice, I knew that it was one of the neighbors that lived next door to Grandpa Ratko. My dad's voice dropped; he took a deep breath and said that he was coming over. It felt like a cold dagger stabbed me right through the heart. Dad hung up and called Mom over. I ran crying to him and asked what happened, and he told me that Grandpa was not answering anybody, "They know he is in the house and slept over there, but he won't answer the phone or the door." They did not know whether to break in or not, so they called my dad. I started getting hysterical, "Oh my god, something happened to him!" My mom clutched me to her breast and told me to calm down, while the tears were rolling down her cheeks as well. My dad hugged us and said he would have to try to get to Grandpa while there was still a slight possibility of helping him. He made a few phone calls and said that one of the neighbors was going with him. They would take the backroads in hopes that they wouldn't run into extremists. He also had some money with him, hoping to bribe them, if necessary, to pass through safely. Dad also spoke to the TO, and they would help him get in and out. I stared at him, knowing this could be the last time I saw him, but my heart did not want to believe that. He packed a little bag and left quickly. My mom went to him as he left, and he whispered something in her ear. Her face just got worse, but she tried to hide it quickly from me. My mom could not say anything to him, but I knew she wanted him to stay. Ratko was his dad, however. His only parent. We all knew he needed to go. Once he left, my world just got worse.

After several hours, we had still not heard from him. Even with the barricades, we knew that it didn't take that long to get there and see what happened. Mom and I were fearing the worst. She paced the room back and forth, and I just pretended to watch TV. The worst thoughts were going through my mind. I knew something terrible had happened to Grandpa. I was praying that I could see him again and tell him how much I loved him and that I would be with him always. I hoped that my dad would bring him back, so he didn't have to be alone again. I wished that I would have listened to him and stayed with him more than with my friend's parents as babysitters. The guilt was killing me.

In this situation, no news was worse. I had a knot in my stomach. *I felt I had failed my grandpa.* That's all that was going through my head. The phone finally rang, and Mom leaped to answer it. She was relieved to hear my dad but was listening intently. He said he was in the hospital with Grandpa. She listened to everything and finally hung up. She started crying immediately, and I cried with her, not even knowing what was going on. She finally grabbed me and tried to calm me down because I could not stop asking what had happened. I could tell that she was holding back tears while on the phone with my dad. She finally told me everything. Grandpa had a brain aneurysm while he was sleeping. Dad had to climb over the neighbor's balcony and break in to find him lying in bed incoherent. "He was irresponsive," Mom said, sobbing. The image came into my mind, and a sick feeling came over me. A real, pure sadness, my heart was crushed.

Mom said they took him to the hospital because there was no telling if an ambulance would even show up. Grandpa was still alive, but he seemed to be in a coma, "Your dad said that he would stay there as long as they let him and try to come back by tomorrow." I was relieved that he was alive, but that is because I did not understand the misery of being in a comma. My world just came crashing down. I had failed my grandpa, and my worst fears were coming true. Grandpa Ratko was alone and, with the stress of this chaos happening, he suffered near death, and I was not there to help him or even be with him. Mom and I held each other, and we sobbed ourselves to sleep.

The next morning, I woke to find people in our house: Mila and her husband, Vedad, and their little boy, Luka. They all came when they heard the news and wanted to console us. They brought over some saved-up lokmas, a delicious fried dough, which was a tradition. They were worried about my dad as well. He had been gone for a full day now, and there was no saying when he would be back. I spent time with Daniel, and he made me feel better. He was, indeed my best pacifier. We had lost all track of time. Even as it started to get dark, we still had no word from Dad. The neighbors all eventually had to leave, and Mom and I had only our anxiety to keep us company, with no more distractions from our friends. I could see by Mom's face that her thoughts were going a million miles an hour, and none of them were good. I could not help but start to feel the same.

Thank goodness it was not too long after that, Dad walked into the door. He looked horrible and pale, worn out with huge, dark circles under his eyes. He still smelled of the hospital. His head was down, and his spirit was gone entirely. I felt his heaviness immediately. We jumped up and ran to him, but all he could do was hug us and put his head on Mom's shoulder. Not one word from him. My anxiety level rushed to my head. My chest was tightening by the minute. Dad separated from us and went to the kitchen and downed a glass of water, then headed to the sofa.

We both sat in silence next to him. He looked to us and shed a tear. That was the first time in my life that I had seen my dad cry. Dad, my hero, now vulnerable, sad, and crying. His voice cracked as he started to explain, "It was tough for me to find my dad like that and see him in that state in the hospital. I was in the room with him, and he was in a coma. Grandpa would mumble at times and, from what I understood, he was saying something about not wanting to die in the war. He did not want to hear the shots. He was mostly unresponsive, but I was right by his side. The doctors said that it was uncertain if he would recover or not." Dad put his head down in sorrow, "In the morning... I thought he was waking up. I was excited to see him do even just that, but Grandpa grabbed the blanket and turned to his side. He used to turn like that a lot when he slept. For just one instant, it was as if he was quietly sleeping at home. Then he turned and, it seemed like he took his last breath. A few seconds later, the monitors went offline, and he was gone."

Dad started to cry again, and I threw myself at him and screamed. I was so angry and upset, I cried out, "It was all my fault!" Grandpa had died alone, his biggest fear. I felt so mad at us for leaving him there. I knew that the fear of war happening had killed him. All that anxiety had stolen my Grandpa from me. It was all my fault; I should have never left him. I should have spent time with him and went to school where I used to go so I could see him every day. I <u>promised</u> him that he would not die alone, and I failed him. He was right about everything. The war was coming, and he did not want to be here for it. "I should have been there and listened to him. I could have saved him." Dad wept as he stammered that the only thing that was bright in my grandpa's life had been me. That I had been the reason, he had lived even this long. Dad tried to assure me that none of it was my fault and that Grandpa was in a better place. He had gone in peace and was better off, but he would always be there watching over me. He told me that he was sure of that.

My dad was always a realist and told me that things happen how they are supposed to. That there was nothing or no one that could change them. We had to accept what happened and go on. His calm words did settle me down a little bit – and I did understand – but still, to this day, I feel like I could have done more for my Grandpa, and maybe saved him. If anything, I could have helped him die with us loving all over him, instead of alone. I will always carry that burden with me. Mom asked when he would be buried, but Dad said that nobody could tell him, because of the situation in the city. "They will let us know. They advised me to go home because it could be a while." My heart was so sad. I cried myself to sleep. It took us six years to find out where Grandpa was buried.

The next couple of days felt like prison again. The neighbors came over to be there for us. I just tried to distract myself from the pain, either by talking to Daniel or playing with little Luka. My heart broke, and I prayed to God that Grandpa would forgive me. The knot in my chest tightened as the situation around us worsened. The shots outside were getting more sporadic, and the food was running out. The news was worse and worse every day. Innocent people were getting killed. There were demonstrations in the streets, people fighting amongst each other and against the police. The violence was crazy. It was confusing what anyone was even protesting. Each religious side was angry with the other. There was no evidence that either side committed any crimes. It was all political, but enraged people couldn't see that. They were blinded and harboring hate. People were starving, which only intensified the anxiety and anger more. Each side was convinced, through propaganda, that they deserved their land for themselves and that other religions were trying to take it.

The police were the enemy on both sides, which I could not understand. The hate was overtaking even the closest friends and neighbors. The houses were getting vandalized, and there was pure chaos. We honestly did not know where we were standing. We were like trapped animals, all that as I was harboring the sadness for my Grandpa. Things got worse and worse until, one day, actual hell was unleashed. The onset of the Civil War in Bosnia: April 2, 1992.

Chapter Five

When it began, my family and I were sitting on the sofa, watching TV. Dad heard unusual noises coming from outside, behind our houses. He went to the small corner of the living room window. It was dusk, but it seemed like there was some movement over at the airport. My dad told me to bring the binoculars that were in their room. I ran and got them, then stood right next to him – ever the curious 10-year-old – as he tried to make out what was happening. I wasn't frightened, yet, because I did not hear gunshots. Dad saw soldiers, many of them, all crawling around the gates of the airport. They were everywhere, and there were tanks too. Then a terrible orange light, "Oh crap. There's a hanger on fire, and it's spreading," he shouted.

He was nervous but assumed the army was there to help the fire. I wanted to see, and he pointed for me, "Quickly look, then get down." I could see the tanks and many soldiers crawling. They strangely looked like they were in a drill, all on the floor crawling with painted faces and camouflaged uniforms. They were carrying rifles and looked like they were taking over the territory to position themselves for an attack. The feeling that came over me was one of dread, and I could feel my dad's energy confirm that feeling as well. I was terrified. The fire was getting bigger by the minute.

It all happened so fast, in a matter of seconds. Dad put his arms around me and pulled me down, away for the window. Then all I remember was a strange rumble and a loud BOOOMMMMM, a ripping and terrifying noise. The force of the blast was so strong that it took my breath away. I was in the air with my dad, floating. The sound continued, but, now, it was also deep inside my body. I felt the force against me. The detonation of a grenade had thrown us against the opposite wall. The boom was so loud that I couldn't hear anything afterward. I was gasping for air from the shock and listened to a low-pitched ringing in my ears, nothing else. In that same instant, the lights went off everywhere. I saw a flash of light and thought I was dead. I fell on the other side of the living room. As I was flying through the air, it all seemed unreal, except that I could feel Dad's arms holding me so tight that I couldn't breathe, but were his arms the reason I couldn't, or was I dying?

All I knew was that I could not feel or hear anything. Dad was saying something, but I could not hear him or respond. He was lying next to me. A grenade fell somewhere close, and it shook the whole house. The walls were still trembling, and I remember trying to breathe. I thought that the entire house was falling on us. Mom was on the floor, screaming and crawling to us. It was so dark that my vision was blurry. I couldn't see or orient myself. Dad turned around next to me and dragged me away out of the living room. Mom was right behind us, her hand on my shoulder. She took a flashlight from the hall as they crawled and dragged me away. More flashes of light were coming from outside, and the rumbling of grenades continued. My dad managed to stand up, and he lifted me to take me down to the basement. Our basement was just a lower level of the house that was still half above the ground. That seemed to be the best for us now, somewhere where there were not that many windows. I was in shock. I was slowly gaining back the feeling in my body, even if I did not want to because I was feeling sore. I also heard better, my ears recuperating. That was when I started to realize everything that had just happened, and I started crying. Mom and Dad were both right next to me. We huddled on the floor next to each other. They were hugging and kissing me, asking me if I was okay. I nodded yes as they checked me all over for cuts. Dad was bleeding from his nose. I ran my hand over my forehead and felt blood running down. I felt pain all over my body, and it seemed wherever I looked, there was some blood. Mom saw this and screamed in fear. My scalp was cut open.

Dad held her back, and then neighbors – who seemed to appear from out of nowhere – grabbed her and calmed her down while Dad scrutinized me. Even in these awful circumstances, he still had his gentle touch and words that gave me comfort, "She is okay. It is just a few scratches." He cleaned the blood with one of the blankets and put a lot of pressure on my head. I was scared, anxious, and hurting. It felt like an alternate universe. All I could think at that moment was, "Thank goodness we're alive." Mom put the flashlight on the dimmest setting, just enough to see but not enough to cause attention. Dad kissed my forehead, "We should stay in the basement for a while. At least until things calm down. We need to bring down food, blankets, and supplies."

Right at that moment, we heard screams and crying. We all recognized the voices as Senka and her kids. Dad stood up and told us that he was going to get them and bring them to the basement. I did not let go of Mom, who was crying and praying under her breath. I told her I loved her, and she told me that everything would be okay, she loved me too.

Minutes went by before Dad came back with Senka and the kids. Senka was frozen in shock. She couldn't talk and could barely walk, and the two boys were terrified. Daniel ran and sat next to me, and we all huddled together. Mom took Senka's hand and made her pray with her. She seemed to respond to that and calm somewhat. Daniel was asking questions, but I could not even gather my thoughts, let alone explain everything that had happened. Mom touched Daniel and signaled with her eyes for him to go to his mom and help her. He seemed to understand and went to be with her.

In my mind, it all was happening fast but also very slow. Looking back, I believe I had a concussion. My dad went back up and got blankets, food, water, and candles. He said that Senka's entire bedroom wall was down and that there were dead men slaughtered in front of her bedroom, probably soldiers that were outside. I couldn't believe my ears, but it certainly helped me to understand why Senka was in total shock. It seemed like a scene out of a war movie, but this was real, and we were in the middle of it. I caught myself hoping I would pass out so that I wouldn't have to experience this anymore but, even though I felt woozy, Mom ordered me not to fall asleep. Instead, she rocked and held me. I was in pain all over, the scratches were still bleeding, and I felt my body very heavy. I felt disoriented as if I was in another world. That was the longest night. The walls kept shaking intensely as grenades continued to fall. The gunshots were constant. We knew nothing, not whether the next missile would hit our house, or if somebody would come in and kill us all. All while I was woozy, but I knew I had to concentrate not to fall asleep. It was terrifying.

The basement was not much of a room, just used for hobbies and storage. It was not very insulated or protective, but it was the safest place in our house. We all knew, however, that – no matter where we were in the house – if a grenade were to fall on it, we would all die. All we could do was sit there and pray to God to spare us. Many grenades fell far away, but some were close enough to shake the walls and scare us to death. That night, I concentrated, and I counted over four hundred fallen grenades before I saw the light of dawn. Mom then told me it was okay to sleep, so I finally dozed off.

When I woke, I had only slept for an hour or so. I couldn't hear any more gunshots or grenades. Everybody was still in the basement except for my dad and Dino. Looking exhausted and worried, Mom told me they went to check out the situation. Senka looked even worse. She still wasn't saying much. When Dad and Dino came back, they said they had spoken to the neighbors. Most of the houses looked torn up, but fixable. All of the neighbors were okay, only sustaining minor injuries. The outside of our house didn't look too destroyed, but there was a smell of smoke and carnage. We didn't know much about casualties, apart from the reports from our immediate houses. Dad said it was okay to go upstairs and gather things up, to get ready for more nights like the one before. I asked him what happened, "The Serbians took over our Army equipment and ammunition and used it to ambush the airport. There were Serbian Eagle flags on the tanks and vehicles. The armed soldiers have bazookas and grenade launchers too." I immediately considered those soldiers our enemies; they were trying to kill us. I asked Dad what they wanted, "To occupy this land, for it to be solely Serbian. In war, the first thing that is worth occupying is the airport, because of the transportation it provides." I asked him if they wanted to kill us. He said he didn't know; that we needed to wait and see. I felt that knot in my stomach again. That was not the answer I wanted to hear.

My body felt a lot better that morning, more focused. I was able to get up and walk. Mom held me up, and we all went upstairs together, where my fears got worse. I didn't know what to expect. We saw all of the damage, a big mess of glass and particles everywhere. It was weird to hear birds singing as if nothing horrible has happened. It was hard for me to walk. I hurt from the fall against the wall. My back and my legs were hurting, and I had cuts everywhere. I limped upstairs and, the closer I got, the more I smelled the smoke and grenade and bullet odors. It stank like death.

That was the first time I realized that, from now on, I had to be a grown-up and be stronger than ever. I think the adrenaline had kicked in because I wanted to see what happened. Mom held me up and never let go of my arm. Our living room was torn up. Everything was on the floor, and the windows were broken. It was a mess everywhere, but the walls were there. All our furniture was full of glass. Our DVDs, videos, even the TV itself were strewn across the floor. It was sad to see how messed up everything was. Dad told us to stay low and away from the window, not to look outside toward the airport. I couldn't help but notice the tanks, each with a Serbian flag on it like Dad said. A weird eagle spread on their red, white, and blue background. They were also playing Serbian folk music on the loudspeakers. Most of them had beards and looked very scary. I put my head down instantly, and we went to the bedrooms to gather stuff. My dad told me to go with my mom. He and Dino took the mattress to cover the window. The others they took downstairs. We could use it for sitting or sleeping in the basement. Mom told me to pack a few clothes and any school stuff that might be useful. We took all the batteries out of everything to use them for what was necessary.

After I gathered my bag, she told me to go to the kitchen and help her bring all the food down to the basement. We only had a few cans of food, a bag of sugar and flour, and a few canisters of cabbage, dried beef, and water. I could not help but notice that it would not be enough food for us, especially since we did not know how long we would have to stay down there. I heard Mom tell Senka to bring all of her food down as well. She also brought down the portable radio and small TV so that we could stay informed about the situation. We took candles and flashlights and a plastic bag she stuffed with the little cash we had, as well as all of our documents.

I realized that the power still had not come back, and I had a bad feeling that it was not going to any time soon. I wondered what the soldiers were up to and why there were no hostilities during the day. I didn't know if they had a method for fighting and occupying the land. I was so confused and scared, but my mind kept telling me that all we could do was stay put and hide. As I was helping pack, my mind could not stop running. *What did our future look like? Did we even have one?*

As the women brought the food, medicine, and water downstairs, the men secured the place by putting extra protection on doors and windows. We were preparing the basement to be our new home, our hiding place from death. The day went by quickly. Daniel was away, helping his mom and brother gather everything to our basement. He would look at me and hug me every minute he had. I told him not to squeeze me too hard because I was in pain. Both of our families were going to stay together, as they decided it was safer. Senka was so grateful because she did not have anybody. She was a single mom with two boys. She kept telling us, "God bless you. God bless you." They were part of our family now. I could see that Dino was very curious about everything. He wanted to go out with a rifle and fight, but Dad told him that this was no joke. Dino could die very quickly. He hugged Dino as if he was his dad too, "The soldiers outside may have some mercy on women and children, but not for furious boy with a rifle." He told him to stay away from the rifle and to be smart. I wasn't sure if Dino was convinced, even though Dad was genuine and very serious.

The day was beautiful outside, not snowing or scorching hot. Thank god. It was still a little cold, so having heavier clothes on was great. We had no ventilators or heaters, so we relied on fresh air and candles, living like cave dwellers. What was scariest was that we knew this was not temporary. We were going to live like prisoners for a while if we survived. I realized that my stuffed bunny was still there, so I grabbed it and just sat there.

We worried as night fell. We had been right to anticipate that the darkness would again bring with it the fall of grenades. The rumbling noise started as we were still going back and forth from the house to the basement. I caught sight of the bright flashes in the background; balls of light I knew were grenades. Just like the one I saw that first night. In an instant, there were ten more all over the sky, and it illuminated the entire area. The noise was getting louder, and the shootings started too. Scared to death, we ran down to the basement, shut the door, and secured everything we could. Mom lit the candles and turned on the radio, trying to find a station that was covering the situation. It was not very long until we heard the firing of grenades and bazookas from the airport. The hard, deep, piercing noise of those machines sounded like the world was coming to an end. We felt so insignificant next to those deadly machines. There was nothing we could do amidst the hair-raising noises and gravity-defying pressure each detonation made. It twisted your stomach upside-down in a knot. That began another long night of brutal grenade spraying, gunshots, and fear.

I hated to think that this could be how I left this world, listening to grenades and then being blown up by one. *Would we be taken prisoner, or hauled into a concentration camp like Grandpa Ratko told me?* My mind could not wrap itself around all of the horrible outcomes we were facing. I would rather die than be imprisoned, I thought. I hoped that God would listen to my prayers; to get us out safe.

A newscaster announced, "Serbian troops are advancing through neighborhoods around the airport, like Dobrinja. They are killing and destroying everything in front of them, imprisoning women and children and killing non-Serbian males." I remember Grandpa telling me that these so-called "guerilla tactics," were the most brutal. The soldiers would burn and kill anything in the way. Any survivors would be either imprisoned or killed. Mom was breathless, and her grip tightened around Senka's hand and me. Dad had a terrified look on his face. I had never seen him like that. I knew he did not have an answer for us. I was scared. My heart was pumping so hard, the adrenaline pumping and making me feel both strong and weak at the same time.

A loud boom shook the whole house, we all trembled in fear at another grenade too close to the house. The candle flickered, and our shadows were like empty ghosts. Every little creak, noise, shot, and missile was so deeply analyzed and feared. We didn't know if every sound, big or small, was a sign of the soldiers coming in to kill us all. The night crawled on, many grenades, countless shots. All we could do was listen and try to learn which piece of heavy machinery was firing by its sound, wondering what each could do. Dad came close and talked to me about everything: the different kinds of grenades, what each did. He explained how to use a rifle in case anything happened, "You know you are meant to grow up and do something great. You need to know how to defend yourself. If you ever need to use a rifle, you need to take it and not think of anything. Just shoot who wants to harm you and make sure they are dead." I remember him trembling, holding the rifle and telling me how to grip it and use it. I couldn't believe how heavy it was, how deathly its nature. I quickly realized the power of the gun. The death that it brought with it. The seriousness of what was out there. So many people using these monstrous guns, "If it is you or another person, you use it. Protect yourself." I was scared and distressed, but I had to be strong for my dad. He hugged me and told me that everything would be okay. He was trying to be my savior.

The next few nights were the same, but now the gunfire continued throughout the day as well. We never felt safe getting out of the basement. The boys would go up to gather blankets and scavenge any food or water they could find. We were prisoners, hoping and praying to survive. The food was running out; there was barely any water left to drink. We only ate one piece of bread with a canned bit of pepper every day. It was great when we were hungry, but it barely satisfied us. Our bodies and minds were growing weaker. Every day I started to daydream more, about food, about being in school, about going to the mountains, seeing my grandpa again, seeing my family again. All of that seemed to be like a dream, so unreal. Some nights I cried myself to sleep, but most nights, I spent the time talking to Daniel. We talked about our memories of school, what we wanted to eat, and how much we would love to play outside. All we had left of our childhood was our imaginations.

Chapter Six

One of the nights, I thought the end of the world was coming. It was early dusk, which was usually when the shootings and grenades started to echo the worst. We were sitting, listening to the shells. That sound still echoes in my head, the sound of falling grenades. At night, that sound was natural, part of my nightly routine, like a violent clock ticking. Those sounds of falling grenades became my lullabies. One night, however, even that awful lullaby was shattered by another even more horrifying and more threatening noise. Out of nowhere, we heard an ear-piercing, earth-shattering rumble. It sounded like the center of the earth was opening up and swallowing everything inside, like nothing I had ever heard. It was so much louder than any bomb. I hysterically clenched onto Mom's arms. I thought we were going to die, right then. Dad came close and told me, "Don't worry, it's just a fighter jet breaking the sound barrier. It's not a bomb." It was so loud because the jet was physically going so fast. I felt better for a bit, but, there were more sounds of aircraft flying over our house, and rockets falling. To this day, when I hear a loud jet, it reminds me of that night that we spent listening to the destruction. The planes continued flying for several hours, destroying our town.

They were coming from the airport, and we knew that they were destroying all of the Muslim and Croat neighborhoods. The radio kept saying, "The jets are Serbian Kamikazes." They also used the term "Chetniks," a word for Serbian extremists. We huddled together and listened to the continuous destruction. I lay across my mom and dad and tried to fall asleep. I was exhausted; my heart was not ready to take all of this; neither was Mom or Senka. They kept praying and rocking back and forth.

We all looked so pale from fear and lack of nutrients. Daniel looked terrified, but Dino was angry. He hit his fists and paced back and forth. I would smile at Daniel and my parents, but I could not look at Dino. Instead, I just turned away toward Mom and started counting the grenades to fall asleep like I usually did. I thought of how incredibly horrible it must feel for my parents and Senka to know that their kids were so near death, and there was nothing they could do about it.

The next morning, however, was surprisingly quiet. I worried that perhaps it was because there was nothing left of our town to destroy. I woke up, and Dad was not there, he had gone upstairs with Dino to see if he could find more food and how much damage there was. I wanted to go upstairs and see it too. Despite Mom screaming after me, I ran up into the house. The outside looked smoky, and the entire neighborhood was in ruins. It seemed half destroyed, with distant houses burning. There was nothing on the streets, just smoke, and dirt. Dad saw me, grabbed me, and told me to get Mom. On the way down, I looked at my bedroom. It was destroyed, the walls were full of holes. Everything was on the floor in a huge mess, and my blue desk had fallen over. All of my belongings and school stuff was everywhere. Like a bomb had gone off inside. I didn't have enough time to gather my emotions or to fully understand that our house and city was slowly getting destroyed, but the harsh reality was there.

Once I had brought Mom back up with me, Dad spoke to us in distress. He told Mom to pack our documents and more clothes to take down. While she did that, Dad found a bag of flour in the kitchen to take down. I asked Dad how my room get so messed up, and he told me to look to the top of the window frame. There were two small holes that I could not even see that well, "Those were special bullets, dispersible little shells that enter anywhere. They are slim but they disburse into millions of pieces and destroy everything." I looked at him, "There are so many things built to destroy." I was getting an education I would never have in school. The knowledge that I wish I had never had.

Suddenly, we heard shots coming from the airport, getting very close to the house. Somebody was watching and shooting at us! Shots blasted through the house, that's all I could hear. It was around us, and I did not know where they were hitting. All I could do was follow my parents. We scrambled downstairs in a panic, running for our lives. Mom and I were screaming. We almost tumbled down the stairs, but we managed not to get shot. Dad was furious, cursing aloud, "Those damn people are trying to kill innocent women and kids." Mom was crying, and I was in such shock that I did not know what to think. The shots stopped, and Mom asked me a hundred times if I was okay. All I could do was nod my head.

The anxiety in the basement was tremendous. We all wondered why we were targets. The fear sank into us, knowing that nobody would have mercy on us. We knew we would get killed here. We lit the candles again and sat down in the basement. I heard my parents and Senka talking, while Daniel held me. He was telling me that everything would be okay, but all I could focus on was what the adults were saying, "We need to try to get out of here. They will come to get us. We need to see if we can talk to the Serbians at the airport into at least letting the women and children go safe or try to make a run for it." Mom was crying and saying that she would not leave without Dad. He just hugged her and kissed her forehead. I turned to Daniel and put my head on his shoulder and started crying. I can't even describe how it felt, knowing that we were waiting there to die. That death was almost inevitable. It was just a matter of when and how.

Your mind, at some point, goes numb as a defense mechanism. At that point, all that mattered was my family. I wondered how the rest of them were doing. *Were they dead? Or suffering like us?* I thought of Grandpa and, for a moment, found comfort in the idea that at least I would see him again soon. My body was going numb too. I held on to my parents. Dad was contemplative about how to save his family, while everyone else was just numb like me. We were all hungry, but none of us could think of food while our adrenaline was running high in hopes of survival. That night continued in horror like any other. There were grenades and bazookas, jets flying, and countless shootings. We huddled and listened to the radio, dialing from one station to another as the horrible reports droned on endlessly. One side was blaming the other for the crimes.

That is how we spent the next few days and nights. During the day, we were shot at by the airport soldiers. We were getting used to being living targets, trying to keep each other calm and give each other some hope. If one of us cracked, the others would lift their spirits. If one of us was on the edge of going crazy, Dad was there to calm them down. It was hard because we barely had a glass of water a day to drink. Our bodies were weak because we did not have any food. We ate canned meat like dogs. I remember eating the same can for days among all of us, something like Spam or corned beef. It was cold and nasty, but it was all we had to keep us alive. The lack of food was nerve-wracking, as we all grew grumpier and more scared. Our food, water, and patience were spread thin. I knew Dad and Mom were plotting to escape. I would spend most of the day talking to Daniel. We always went back to using our imaginations, we reminisced about school days, playing word games, and thinking of the travels we took. Thank goodness I had him and my parents, and my stuffed bunny because being stuck in between those four walls was insanity.

It was hard to keep track of time, but I believe it was the middle of June when another misery added to our situation. We were spending the entire day in the basement, except for Dad and Dino, venturing up to assess the situation. Sometimes, Dad even got out to communicate with other neighbors or the TO, especially to see if there was any more food. TO had secret tunnels to travel with more guns, water, and food to help us countrymen survive. They continued to become so much more than a Muslim army.

Dad also tried to see if there was any way out of the neighborhood, to at least send Mom and me out. He and Dino would get items from the sewer tunnel the TO used to transport goods. That was our lifeline, as we had nothing to survive on. One day, as we waited for them to return, we heard more gunshots that seemed to be aimed at us again. All around us, the shots were hard and noisy and scary. Suddenly, Dad came running into the basement, but Dino was not with him. Senka started screaming, "Why is he not with you!?!" He was confused, saying that he had told Dino not to go out with him at all today, "I told him to stay with you." I stood in panic. My heart almost stopped beating. He told everyone to stay down and that he would go up to find him. It seemed like forever that he was gone as we held down panicking Senka, but eventually, we couldn't stop her running upstairs too. Mom and I held Daniel, and stayed there, following Dad's orders. I was crying, panicking, and then we heard a scream from Senka. "Oh my god! Oh, my lord, noooooooooooo!" We knew something was wrong. I heard Dad talking, but we could not hear Senka anymore.

I took Mom's arm and told her that we needed to go up, but she would not listen. She pulled me back, but I was determined. We needed to help, I told her. We went up slowly, looking for Dad and Dino. They were not in the house, but we saw an attic door open. I called up to Dad, but all we heard was Senka's deep sobbing. Once we found him, Dad told us to get downstairs right away. We obeyed, and it was not long before he returned, holding Senka, and Daniel was by their side.

They both looked like ghosts. Senka was shaking beyond control; her eyes fixed on the floor. She looked like a crazy person, her head wavering back and forth, talking to herself. It almost sounded like she was praying, but we could not make out what it was. Daniel held her tight, his eyes full of tears and horror on his

---

46

face. We ran right up to them. Mom sat Senka down, but she was not responding. I asked what had happened, and Dad told us that we needed to give Senka some water and also sugar if we had any at all. Daniel stayed silent and just kept crying from the bottom of his heart. Seeing his tears hurt me so much that all I could do was cry with him.

Dad said to take care of them and that he would be right back. Mom brought Senka water, held her hand, and prayed with her as best they could. We did not know what was happening, but could only assume that it was Dino. I tried talking to Daniel, but my best friend was so angry that he pushed me away and did not want anything to do with me. I knew then that this had broken him.

Above us, I heard Dad open the front door. I peeked up the stairs and saw my dad carrying Dino, and I could tell immediately. He was dead, a lifeless weight in my father's arms. I could not believe he was gone. That image still burns in my head, his skin gray and bloody, a hole in his head.

I ran back down the stairs and fell to my knees. I could not feel my legs. I felt nauseous and dizzy. I started crying, crawled next to Mom, and continued to pray. I did all I could to block the image out of my head. Dad returned right before dusk. He looked sad but calm. I ran to him, but Mom stayed with Senka. Dad told us that it looked like Dino had been using the little window in the attic. He was curious and looking through binoculars toward the airport, and the soldiers shot him in the head. They saw him moving in that little oval window, the binoculars glinting in the sun. They must have thought that he was a sniper from TO, and shot him.

My breath was knocked out of me, listening to this. This innocent child was murdered. Dad looked angry, stressed, and out of hope. He said that this was probably why the soldiers were shooting at us, at the house, because they thought we had someone shooting at them. TO was sneaking around and taking shots at the Serbs. That did not help the situation either. The Serbs had no mercy. They just shot if someone was shooting at them. He had gone to talk to the TO, and they took the body. They said they would make sure nobody went into our neighborhood, and that they would take care of the body, offering condolences to Dino's family.

The TO had trucks to pick up corpses and take them away. Dad told us all of this quietly, so Senka did not hear it. My body was shutting down. *So many people were dying that there was a truck picking up corpses? Could we escape on that truck away from here? Could we talk to the TO army to save us? Would Senka ever see where they bury him?* My mind was racing, but my mouth was so numb that not a single mumble was coming out. Even though I was silent, Dad spoke to all of this, "We will not know where they take the body, but it can't stay here. There is a shortage of graves, and there is no way we are getting out of here anytime soon. Soldier camps surround us." I don't know how he knew to answer all my questions; I guess the expression on my face said it all.

Dad and I went over to Mom and Senka and hugged them. Senka looked bad. She was not saying a word, just rocking back and forth and looked like a ghost. She was not responding to Dad, or even Daniel, who went into my dad's arms and cried. Daniel tried to punch him, but Dad just held him and comforted him. He knew that Daniel was just angry, and Dad was a father figure to him.

I could not believe that, just like that, Dino, gone forever. I had no idea how Daniel and Senka would survive their grief, or if any of us would survive any of this. I knew we needed to do something. This could not be the end of our lives. I was so confused, scared, hungry, hurt, and anxious. All these emotions were so intense, and we were all victims of this dark reality. All I could do was cry and pray and stay in Mom and Dad's arms.

Our hurt, sorrow, and anger were getting overwhelming. The shootings continued all the next day, which kept us imprisoned and scared. Senka still said nothing, but Daniel had gotten a little better. He even came over and hugged me. I did not know what to tell him; we sat in silence. We were all hurting physically, from the discomfort of the basement, the hunger, and thirst. We were hurting emotionally much more; it was awful — the anguish of a lost one and nothing we could do. The image of lifeless Dino kept popping up in my head, and it was almost unbearable. We ate canned peppers, only two for each of us. At least Senka ate. Dad was trying to figure out what to do. Daniel was the only thing keeping Senka alive. She finally spoke, asking Dad what had been done with Dino's body. It was horrible to see her face as Senka absorbed the information that he didn't know. She kept crying and holding Daniel. Mom hugged her as we listened to grenades and the same old news about destruction. We spent the next days and nights in sorrow and despair.

Chapter Seven

Dad informed us that TO was not able to help us get out for right now, but they were working on it, at least they helped with food and weapons. Mom asked if there was anything we could do, how we could get out. They spent a lot of time talking and contemplating how to improve our situation. TO hesitated to help Dad because of his Serbian name— the same TO that helped him before was now skeptical. That was the first sign that we truly needed to do something because the only help we had was slowly diminishing. He said that they had been difficult with the body, but took it because Dino was a Muslim. What helped Dad was that he made a few good friends in the TO army an those few continued to help. TO was starting to forget about being a 'peoples' army.' Everybody was getting segregated.

That was the worst part. Hatred spreading like a plague that infected fast. We did not know what we could do or whom we could trust. Mom was terrified. The odds of us dying here were increasing by the minute. My parents considered everything, but any plan seemed too dangerous. I sat next to Daniel and hugged him, telling him that we would figure a way out. He just lowered his head and said that he wanted to see Dino again, that he wanted to tell him that he loves him. Dino had been like his father – a mentor – and he lost him just like that.

After a while, Mom and Dad had an idea that could perhaps get the women and children out. I automatically told Mom that I was not leaving without Dad. I was hysterical, but Dad took my hands and told me, "We need to try to talk to the soldiers at the airport and see if we can solve things peacefully. I don't believe they're there to kill innocent people. Their mission is to hold territory. TO says they haven't been killing people and have even been negotiating on certain terms with

---

TO. They don't want to kill women and children." I could tell by his tone that he was still skeptical, but he knew that we had to try something. Daniel stood up, "I'm not going over there and begging from the people that killed my brother. I'd rather stay here and die and maybe kill a few of them with me." I was shocked. I looked at Daniel, my best friend, and couldn't even recognize him. The hatred had gotten to him too. Though I could understand the feeling, he had lost his brother.

Dad explained that this was our only option to stay alive. The plan worried Senka, and she didn't seem willing to cooperate until Dad said that it was the one idea that could keep Daniel alive. We had no other choice. Hearing this, she agreed. Dad turned to all of us, "Those soldiers would have killed us a long time ago if they wanted to. They are not there to do that. They want the territory." He had to remind us, no matter how painful it was, that the soldiers killed Dino because they thought that he was a TO sniper. He kept reassuring us that everything would be fine. We needed to take this chance and try something.

Eventually, we all agreed. So, that night, we planned what we needed to say and how to approach them. My dad didn't sit down all night, let alone sleep. He was worried, and I knew he could not live with himself if anything happened. I knew, however, that we needed to trust him. I stayed up all night with him, as well. We all did, dozing off and on, but together we waited for morning daylight.

The next morning, we were all anxious. Dad was looking more worried, and Senka and Daniel looked like they were going into a boxing fight. I had to admit that I was beside myself, but something inside me told me to trust Dad. We hugged Dad tight as he said to us that everything would be okay. It was on July 7th, we all left the basement, and the house itself, to venture out into plain sight. We walked down the middle of the road to the airport.

The place looked like a scene from a sci-fi movie, featuring us walking into a death trap. It was a quiet morning, with no gunshots or grenades in the near vicinity. We left the house, went around to the back, and started moving very slowly toward the soldiers at the airport. We were in the middle of the street, holding each other's hands. There was no one around, not even an animal. Everything was abandoned, gloomy, and smoky. It was scary and depressing, but the only thing I could focus on was the overwhelming beating of my heart. All I was thinking about was looking forward to a time when I wasn't thinking about getting shot or being assassinated by soldiers. We kept walking forward, Mom's hands holding mine tight. Her face was getting more worried. I couldn't help but notice stains of blood on the streets, the ruins, and dust, metal dumpsters with holes in them. Smoke and gloominess were everywhere — holes in the buildings, scary-looking guns, and launchers all over the airport.

It was not long before two military vehicles quickly drove toward us, machine guns already pointed right at us. We all froze, my heart in my throat. As they got close, I couldn't help but notice that the soldiers were regular people, most of them with long beards and grins on their faces. They got out and eyed us. They were looking at my mom like a prize but quickly focused on us, the children. Their leader was short with a dark beard, skinny and very loud. He approached and asked what we were doing. The other soldiers stared after him. I couldn't have spoken a word, even if I was supposed to. I have no idea how my mom said anything. I could tell she was as afraid as I was by the way I felt her heartbeat in our tight handhold. She gathered her courage, however, and lifted her head to speak, "Greetings, gentlemen. In our neighborhood, there are only innocent women, children, and elderly. There is no enemy there or anyone that will fight or present harm for you. We need help. We are running out of food and water and would like to help our kids grow up. We want to escape with our children so that you can have the territory you would like. Please, please, please help us." As she pleaded with them, she couldn't help but start crying. That automatically made us all cry as well. I held Mom tighter and stood with her, though both of us stood in fear.

The soldiers just laughed, " We don't have any use for you, and there is nowhere to go. We can maybe use you as whores and slaves." He turned to his soldiers, and they all laughed like pigs. Then he came closer to Mom and said, "We will not hurt you. But we can't help you. You are on your own. If you want to get out, it's on your luck and means." Then he waved his hand toward our entire neighborhood, "This land will be "Code Zero". Now go back and hide and may God be with you."

We were all in shock and so scared, but we heard him loud and clear. The soldiers went to their vehicles, and we turned around and started walking back toward the house. Mom held my hand so hard as we walked faster and faster. I could hear the soldiers laughing, even over my pumping heart, "We can use them as practice targets later on." My knees were giving in, but, since we were all holding hands, I had enough support not to fall. I asked Mom, "What does 'Code Zero' mean? What is going to happen?" She just kept walking until we got to the house, knocking and shouting for Dad to open up. That walk seems like a fantasy to me now. One minute we were walking out there and talking to those soldiers and the next we were back. Though the information we came back with was terrifying. That was when we all started to worry and panic more for our very lives.

Mom ran to my dad and hugged him, crying. He was trying to get her to speak clearly and tell him everything. I attached myself to both of them, never wanting to let go. Dad was getting furious. He was mad at himself for letting us go out there into danger. I know that he still questions himself about doing that, "At least they will not harm us yet, but that tells us that we need to move soon." Senka and Daniel were terrified. They did not say anything. All I could think of was this new phrase that still gives me goosebumps: "Code Zero." I asked Dad what it meant, "It means that they will destroy the whole neighborhood, burn it down, and it will be leveled – bringing it to 'zero level.' " My heart stopped. I told him, "They can't do that with us here! Oh my god, they will kill us all!" Daniel was so frightened that he collapsed to his knees. Senka just stood there, as if all life had just drained out of her. She did not care anymore. She has given up already.

Dad sat us all down, "We need to calm down and figure this out. We will get out on our own." I trusted Dad – call that either innocence or stupidity – but my anxiety was built around survival and not sorrow. I tend to be a positive person. I have no idea how I could have been then, but I guess a human heart can find a positive way somehow, even in the worst situation. Dad sat next to me then and told me one of the most amazing phrases I've ever heard, one that has stayed with me my entire life, "There is always something good, even in the worst situations. Find and focus on the positive."

I spent the night next to Daniel, holding his hand and my bunny and telling him that we would be all right. I tried to meditate on the good: *that we were alive, bonding and learning about how valuable life is.* I focused on loving my family and friends, and it helped me through that night and the next day, which came with the usual noises of gunshots. News stations reported, neighborhoods destroyed by fire, and children and women transported to camps, men of different religions killed, while those of the same faith were forced to fight. I spent the next night counting grenades, my usual sleep aid, my lullaby. My parents stayed awake, talking about how to escape. I fell asleep on Daniel's shoulder.

The next morning was quiet; there were only grenades in the distance and occasional shots in our vicinity. We felt like prisoners in our neighborhood, doomed to stay there and die, but Dad was determined to get us out. We were fatigued, running out of water, and all the food that was left was sugar, vegetable cans, and a few pieces of dry beef. Senka was not looking good. I think she was silently going insane. She was like a zombie with no will for anything. Daniel tried to keep her hopes up, and she would hug him without saying a word. He was scared. He had lost his brother and was now losing his mom. I hugged him tightly. We kept holding each other.

Mom came to me that night and kissed me. She held me tight and told me that she would never let anything happen to me, "God is on our side." That is all we had left: hope, faith, each other, and a belief that miracles would help us. I thought about Grandpa Ratko, and I hoped he had forgiven me: that he was happy in heaven. I hoped Mom's family was okay. I wondered how she was taking it, not knowing how her family was, but there was no time to think about that in our situation. We just hoped that everybody was alive.

The next few nights steadily got more dangerous and unstable. The grenades were vicious, shaking the walls. The shots were constant and very close. The planes continuously roared back and forth above us as bazookas and tanks blasted all around. Though the loud sounds had become normal to our ears, they did not lose their intensity and created fear every time they came close. That night, we heard a loud banging on the door and children crying. Dad grabbed the gun and went to the door. My heart was in my throat until Dad came back quickly with little Luka and his family. Their skins were blackened from the smoke. Luka was screaming, and his parents were terrified. Dad assured them that they were safe. They had escaped their house as it burned down. We gave them some of the little water we had, helped them clean up, and put blankets around them.

Even though it was hot outside, and we had no electricity or air, they were shivering. I guessed this was mostly because of fear. We gave Luka a little water and tried to calm him down. His mother was terrified but focused on her little son. His father, Vedad, talked to mine, saying that their house was shot at and caught on fire. The fire spread quickly, and they had to go out. They told us that the soldiers were burning the whole neighborhood down, a guerilla tactic. They were going down the street and destroying and occupying the district.

They lived only a few blocks down. One phrase popped back into my head: "Code Zero." They were destroying all the houses in the neighborhood. Consumed with worry, Dad, told them how lucky they were that they had not gotten shot running here. They said that they kept close to the houses, hoping the dark would cover them. It sounded awful, "The shots are so constant. You feared the snipers would shoot you immediately." The Serbs had snipers set up everywhere, who wait for their targets. "There is no escaping the precision of a sniper," said Vedad.

We all just sat there in despair, knowing that we were next. We were all terrified. There is no way to explain the feeling of knowing you will die soon and waiting to see how terrible that death would be, all while trying to remain calm. I don't wish it upon anybody. Dad asked Luka's family if they knew of other survivors. They said that the neighbors across the street – Boris's family – were still there, but we didn't know how many more people were left alive in the entire neighborhood.

I could not imagine that other neighbors were gone. Dead. Little old ladies, children, and families that lived right beside us. Our mouths dropped open in despair. There was complete silence for just a moment, as little Luka finally calmed down. We all settled down, but we were beyond terrified. We did not know when they would come for us. The candles flickered and the night finally quieted down. Dawn was coming, but all of us were too anxious and scared to sleep. I played with Luka until the morning. He was sweet and, in some ways, brought some joy and laughter to that basement. He liked my stuffed bunny as well. He did not know what was happening. He was simply a child.

We all just wished to be removed from this situation that it could be over. The day continued with more challenges instead. We were close to death, with more mouths to feed and less room. It all seemed unreal. To this day, I am not sure how we took all of that and kept our sanity. I guess you discover what a human mind was capable of when it is genuinely in turmoil. It all seemed like a bad dream with no ending. We spent those days in anguish and discomfort. Everyone looked like they were in hell. We only had one loaf of bread, a few cans of food, and a bucket of water to share. We were all sluggish, tired, and sickly looking. We were getting cranky and a little insane. I would burst into uncontrollable laughs, followed by crying. We all knew that, if grenades didn't kill us, death would come from hunger or thirst.

It was tough for all of us to be down there. The nights were hot. The silence was beyond uncomfortable. There was an unspoken truth about what happened to Luka's family and what was waiting for us. Dad and Mom tried to ration things out and make a plan. All night we heard the grenades, bazookas, and shots getting stronger. As horrible as the sounds were, they had a calming effect, as they had become the norm for us.

Chapter Eight

One night, the final terror came. We were sitting down listening to the radio. The walls were shaking, and we heard shots that sounded close like they had hit the building. Before we knew it, we smelled smoke in the basement. Within seconds, the room started to fill with smoke, coming from the pipe that leads upstairs. We all started to panic and cough as it got harder to breathe. I was screaming for Mom, who was crying and choking just like me. I was terrified and thought we were going to die. Mom told me to spit in my shirt to make it wet. I was able to breathe better and filter the air through that for a little. I was so scared. All I could see was Mom and Dad holding me and trying to help me breathe. All of us were choking, and Luka was screaming so loud.

Smoke and the smell of burnt concrete filled the room. To this day, whenever I smell anything burning, I start to panic. We knew that we were going to die if we did not leave that house but also that, if we get out, we would most likely get shot and die anyway. In my heart, I knew this was the day we were all going to die. Mom and I cried hysterically. I could not see or hear anyone. All I felt was Mom gasping for air, more and more. My eyes were watering, and I started to feel lightheaded and nauseous. The smoke was thick and deadly.

All of a sudden, I felt Dad's arms around me. He pulled Mom and me with him upstairs toward the front door. I don't remember how we made it up or how we saw anything, because I was fighting unconsciousness. Dad flung open the front door, and we were able to get some air in our lungs. Outside, the noise was terrifying. Grenades illuminated the pitch-black sky, we could hear the crackling of the fire, and see orange flames upstairs. The smoke was thick, but the little air coming in helped us survive. I coughed so loud that I thought my lungs were going to fall out. I couldn't get a deep breath. We gasped and choked; our eyes were bloodshot. It's terrifying, not being able to breathe.

My adrenaline was running. Dad told us that we had to cross the street, to try and make it to the basement of Boris's family. We needed to go as fast as our legs could carry us, and to stay toward the shadowy edge of the street. I was shocked that he still had the strength to lead us. He told us to run in a zigzag, to make it harder for snipers. I saw the pain and suffering in his face. His look said to us that we were risking our lives going out there, but, "If we stay, we will die." He looked worried, telling Mom and I that he loved us very much. Then he shook me, "Do you remember what you have to do? You can do this, honey. I love you." Senka and Daniel were already running out and crossing the street. I thought to myself that the road is not that big. We can make it.

Then Luka's family went. First, his mom and then his dad with the screaming child. Right when they were a third of the way across, Dad kissed me and pushed me forward. He yelled for me to run. It all seemed so fast and unreal, but it was happening. I was on the street, a target, so close to death. I ran in hysterics, across the dark street. All I could hear were sniper shots. I ran in the zigzag pattern Dad told me to, but all the while, I did not know if I was shot or going to make it. There was nothing else to do but run and hope you survive. My mind went numb.

I was operating, running. The wind and the flashing lights were a slight reminder that I was still alive and that I could feel things. Somewhere between the gunshots and my harsh breathing, I heard Mom shouting behind me, telling me to run, but I knew I could not look back. It all was happening as if I was in a surreal movie, a twilight zone. Everything slowed down for me. Still, to this day, I was not sure why. I could see bullets flashes passing all around me but never close to me. I felt as if I had a protective bubble around me, and the bullets never hit me. I felt like I was floating, being guided, and protected. All I did was to focus on running to the other side.

The grenades hit buildings and illuminated the way. During those quick flashes, I could see Luka and his dad in front of me. The shots were getting more numerous, and all I can remember is running for what it seemed like an eternity. As I ran, I heard Luka screaming louder. I stumbled upon the boy on the ground. His father, Vedad, was beside him, holding his side in agony. I don't know where the strength came from, or what made me make that decision, but I grabbed the child as his dad pushed him toward me.

I took Luka as a reflex. I still don't know how I did it. It seemed like it was somebody else inside me doing that. After all, I was just a child myself. I took Luka and kept running as dad had instructed me. I was scared. I did not know what happened to Luka's dad. All I knew was that I had to run for my life toward Boris's house. I did not even feel the weight of his little body. I wanted to live, wanted to make it across the street.

As I ran, I could no longer hear Luka's screaming, nor the shots. I focused on getting to Boris's door. It was as if I went deaf for a minute and just kept going, hoping that I was still alive. The entrance to the house was around back. As I got closer, I heard people calling for me. Another grenade illuminated the sky, and that's when I saw Senka, Daniel, and Boris – our neighbor – waving me toward them. Daniel and Senka made it. I finally got there and rushed inside with the boy. His mother came over immediately and grabbed me. My legs felt so heavy, and I was barely breathing. They took Luka, and I felt relieved, noticing how hard I had been clutching him to my chest. I gasped for air, still numb and in shock.

I turned to see if my parents were coming. I needed them. Thank goodness that, in no time, Mom hurried in behind me followed by Dad carrying Vedad,

Luka's father. I was so happy to see them. I rushed over, screaming for Mom, and she hugged me so hard. I was so glad to see that Luka's dad was alive. I started shaking. My legs gave out, and I collapsed when I reached their basement. I did not know how I made it or how we survived without getting shot. Mom held me while Dad checked me all over.

Our skin was black from the smoke, but I finally started breathing better – even if the cough was still heavy. Mom cleaned my face with a rag and held me. Daniel and Senka sat by my side. Daniel smiled at me, and my life felt better for a moment. We had made it across alive, but I could still smell that awful smoke, the burning of concrete, and everything else. Dad and Boris treated Vedad, who was moaning in pain. I was worried. I asked Mom if he was going to be okay, and she told me that a bullet had grazed him. He was in pain, but he didn't lose his color. He still looked normal. Vedad's scar looked nasty and bloody. His wife was crying over him while holding Luka and calming him down. That's when it hit me. Vedad was shot right in front of me. That could have been me. That could have been any one of us. I could feel his pain. The thought made me feel horrible, but at that moment, Mom reassured me with her hug. She also said how amazing I was saving Luka and whispered to me that she knew the angels were around me, protecting me. " I could see the light around you, guiding you, and protecting you." She hugged me and said everything would be okay. I found comfort in those words and her embrace.

Boris and his wife had another couple there. They were all seated around us, looking scared and full of despair. Mom was quiet. She looked truly sad. Boris's basement was more prominent than ours, but we still felt like sardines trying to survive. They had small, wooden bunk beds, with bricks set up as beds and a mattress as well. Their basement had a tiny round window on each side. Looking around made me realize how we had just escaped death, and that we did not know how long it would be until another encounter was coming. We were very shaken up, smoke still in our lungs and black spots on our skin. Then, orange light from the front window caught my eye. I was still coughing, so Mom did not let me out of her arms, but I dragged her toward the small window.

I approached and pulled myself up. I saw the raging flames consume our house. The entire building was on fire and burning intensely, smoke billowing out of it. There was nothing we could do. There was not enough water to drink, let alone put out a fire. The smoke seemed to carry away all of my memories and belongings into the sky. The only thing we had with us was a small bag we had packed with some extra clothes and our documents and money. Everything else was disappearing in flames. I left my bunny there too as we ran out, I knew then that this was the beginning of the end of my childhood. I could not believe it; my eyes filled with tears. I started coughing, then choking from sadness. Mom was weeping as well. I felt her heavy heart, and I buried my head in her embrace. Dad hugged us with a terrible look on his face but kissed us on our foreheads. We all hugged and cried as our house, and everything we worked for, burned away forever.

Vedad seemed to be doing okay. Dad said he needed medical attention and some antibiotics, and that he would try to get them from TO. Senka was utterly gone; she did not even want to talk. Daniel came up to me, he didn't say a word, but he didn't have to. I knew how he felt. He was so scared for his mom. I laid down on the mattress while everybody else went to the bunks or used the bricks to rest. That night I hardly slept. All I could see in my head was the smoke and orange flames choking and killing us. Like it was not enough to live through the nightmare, now I had to dream about it as well. The night dragged on forever as the guns and bazookas continued. All of us couldn't stop coughing. Vedad groaned in pain.

Dad sat up all night, talking to Boris and checking Vedad's wound. When I caught a glimpse, it looked horrible. It was huge and getting infected. He did not look good at all, and the smell of the wound was terrible. I felt awful for him and his family. I cried silently. Luka had calmed down and was asleep in his mom's arms. She was in distress. I can only imagine how she felt, watching her husband wounded. In her sorrow, she still took the time to come over to me and say, "Thank you for being such a brave girl and saving my boy." She hugged me tightly. I shed a tear of joy and pride for a moment and smiled, but quickly was reminded of our horrible situation by the grenades blasting outside mercilessly.

All I remember next was the morning sunlight coming through the small windows. I must have eventually fallen asleep. The basement looked even tinier in the morning. We were all crowded, and it smelled horrible in there. I woke up with back pain, but the first thing I did was go to the little front window and look outside toward the house. It was charred and destroyed, all gray and black. I could still smell the burning concrete and feel the layer of choking smoke. The skies looked hazy, but it was surprisingly quiet. I could not believe that everything was gone. I turned around, and the room seemed so sad, everyone was losing hope. I started the day crying and remembering our new house and my parent's hard work to get it. I was just grateful we were alive. The only thing to look forward to was survival.

Chapter Nine

The days continued like that. I mostly played with Luka. Daniel and I would talk a lot about school and games that we invented, like naming all the mountains, rivers, and guns we knew. We were exhausted and starving. I remember, a few days after the fire, Boris's wife offered me "something to eat." It was just mixed flour and water. I looked at her with disgust and told her that I was not hungry; it looked horrible. The next day I woke up with extreme pains in my ribs, as I realized that they were sticking out and hurting me on the hard bricks and floor. We were all getting very skinny. I wondered what happened to that little chubby girl. We all looked so different; we had aged so much. We had no toilets, no running water, the smell of urine and feces was horrible, because we had to use the buckets and pour them outside. It was terrible.

The hunger was getting harder to sustain. The next day, when Boris's wife offered me the flour and water, I took it and ate it like it was lobster and steak. The trick was to imagine what you wanted to eat, and you could almost taste it. Daniel and I helped each other imagine good food even when we ate pickles, flour, and water. Occasionally, Dad and Boris would go for a day and find us pieces of bread to share from TO. The nights were getting more dangerous, with grenades falling more often and a lot closer to where we were. We had no escape. Even the days were risky. The radio reported massacres everywhere. The soldiers were taking everyone to concentration camps or killing them. We often heard tanks outside that could destroy the house. The snipers were everywhere, and the planes kept dropping bombs. We could only cower there and wait for our destiny.

My parents never gave up, however. Dad used the TO satellite phones whenever he could. Although I did not know any details, I knew Dad was making a plan. He was talking to our friends in Dobrinja and exploring the situation, using any connections he could to get us out. He did not talk about it much with me, but he and Mom were planning. I just tried to keep my mind off the hunger and fear. Daniel and I kept playing with Luka. That was the best way to cheer up because he was so young and innocent. He smiled, no matter what. It helped us forget what was happening around us.

Vedad was recovering okay. What helped most was the medicine TO gave Dad. He did not have to go to TO quarters, which was available to people that were critically injured but was a possible suicide trip. It was a military truck that transported dead bodies. Injured people would hide in there to get to the doctors and hospitals. We called it "The Death Truck." It went through Serbian zones and dangerous sniper areas, and sometimes they did not make it out. It was the only way, however, to get the medical help that we did not have in the houses. The nights and days continued to be severe, but just when I thought it could not get any worse, another night of horror came.

We were all sitting, listening to the grenades. It was dark, and they seemed very close to the neighborhood. I was right next to Luka and Daniel next to the back window. We were close to each other, getting scared. I felt paranoid. I knew something was going to happen. Right then, a grenade fell right by the back window. The BOOOOOOOOOM was so loud and powerful. The explosion blew so strong that the entire basement shook and the walls cracked around us. My ears were ringing. There were raging flames just outside. The fear of the house burning was so intense that my breath stopped. We were all terrified and couldn't take another escape from a burning house. We did not think that we would be that lucky twice.

I heard Dad yelling that the grenade hit a car parked next to the house. The explosion was horrendous. But, the smell of gas that was coming from the car was terrifying. The flames were intense. I looked at Daniel and Luka, covered in dust, and then I saw that I was too. When I went to shake it off, I realized how much all of the debris hurt. I had pieces of glass all over me. The little window had shattered all over us. I was in pain, tiny glass needles all over my body. I started crying, but my cry was so tame compared to the screaming from little Luka. He was covered as well. Mom was hyperventilating, holding me and trying to take the glass out. Small spots of blood were coming out of my pores. The same thing was happening to poor little Luka.

Then again, the gas had caused another explosion, and we all quaked with fear. The walls shook, but God did not let them crumble. Dad was scared, and Mom was crying, but they were both by my side, holding me. The gas smelled strong, but there were no more explosions. I felt sick to my stomach, though I wasn't sure if it was from the glass or the gas smell or just disgust in the situation. Dad told us all that the worst was over, that the flames would not come close to the house because the car was far enough away. Sure enough, the fires were still burning, but we felt very little smoke as the wind seemed to be enough to spread it outside. My adrenaline kept me shaking. Luka was still crying as his mom cleaned his body.

Boris, his wife, and Luka's parents were all around us, trying to help. They were untouched because they were on the other side of the basement. I couldn't believe that a little window like that could produce so many pieces of glass, but it did. I felt sick to my stomach. I was shaking, and the whole room felt like it was spinning. I felt numb. I think I blocked out a lot of that night because all I remember was waking up and having the blood wiped off of Luka, Daniel and me. We covered the window with wood that used to be a part of the bed. My arms and stomach felt sore, and I had scrapes all over me. I must have passed out from the shock and fear. Mom and Dad hugged me, and I hugged them back. I made sure

---

that they were not hurt either.

I was horrified to see that Luka was unusually quiet and gray, having lost so much blood. I could not imagine losing someone else, especially someone as innocent as Luka. He was still breathing, though, and his eyes were open, but I could tell he was not doing well. I pulled on Mom's shirt and pointed toward Luka. She promised that we would take care of him. Vedad didn't look good either but was mostly worried about his son. It was a strange feeling. Like we were all ghosts sitting there. We had all lost hope. We were speechless. There were cracks all over the walls, the concrete dust piled in a corner. Grenades were still falling, but we were all alive.

The next morning things seemed to be different. We all seemed more distant. Everyone was quiet, and Luka's parents did not let him out of their arms for one second. Senka was next to Daniel, looking like a coma patient. My parents were right next to me. We all felt the same way, wanting to be quiet and reflect on our thoughts. I wanted to be in a better place, and my imagination was the only way. I tried to erase everything and start over, and I felt sorry for myself and everyone else. I was losing hope, as well. The shots were sporadic and the day went by as usual. The few bites of flour and water did the trick to keep us alive, but we had no energy for anything. Before I knew it, morning came again, but there was nothing usual about that morning.

I slept on one of the bunk beds and woke up to the strange sight of Mom sitting next to me. Alone. Everyone else was gone. The morning was quiet, not a sound of a single shot or grenade. It was heavenly calm. The sun was glowing in the small window, and I could smell the grass because the basement door was open. I panicked, but Mom said not to worry, and that the morning was so quiet that everyone was outside enjoying it. I was surprised. She seemed so happy that it felt like the war had stopped for a minute, "Come outside." I got up and took her hand and followed her out. She said that we should collect dandelions and that we might be able to get some honey out of it to eat as the others were doing. I smelled the plants, and I heard everyone outside. I thought it was a joke, how can we possibly go outside,? I asked myself. That's when I realized that we all went a little crazy and at that moment, a moment of despair and loss, your mind will make decision for small pleasures even if it meant the doom. Your defense mechanism is seeking for something to hold on to. We simply didn't care any longer and we decided to go outside.

We stuck close to the door, but we were outside on a beautiful August day. The first person I saw was Dad, who ran to me and held my hand. He told me to keep close. I asked if the war was over and he told me, no, but this good day was an improvement. I looked around at the ruins. Only half of the buildings were left. Bullet holes were everywhere. It was depressing and gloomy. It did not look like my neighborhood at all, more like a scene from a war movie.

The only thing that made it better was that it was still a beautiful day, the sky was blue, and the sun was beaming. I noticed a few bullet chambers on the ground and reached out to collect them. They were 12 mils and huge. I asked Dad why there weren't more. I thought the street would be full of them. He told me that a lot of the soldiers and snipers collect them as evidence to count so that they can get paid per hits. They got paid every time they hit the desired target. "Wow, what a dirty thing." He said they did not care who they hit, even women and children. I got frightened, hearing this, "Should we get inside?" He calmed me, "The snipers are not so active during the day, and they seem not to be here, though we still need to be careful."

I examined the shell and realized that one big bullet like this could kill an elephant. I imagined how that huge bullet could split a man in half. The reality hit me that this was no joke. Just one round could do so much. I started to feel worse,

68

but Dad hugged me, "Don't worry, honey. Everything will be fine. We will get out of here." He kissed my forehead, and his eyes comforted me. I was still terrified, but all of us felt the need to risk it all to go outside for a minute and enjoy being out of the basement, enjoying the daylight. It was therapeutic, and we all needed it for our sanity. The wind and the skies made me happy. I saw the grass and the playground where we used to play. The smell of the August weather was marvelous.

All of a sudden, I felt good. Normal, just for a minute, even though there were ruins everywhere and not an animal or soul on the streets. I felt like a little girl again. I remember that day so well and how, for a moment, we all regained a little hope in the worst situation. As I was standing there, absorbing the atmosphere, I saw Boris walk past with dandelions. We smiled at each other. Daniel was sitting in the grass and signaling me to come over. Everyone else, including Mom, was picking any dandelions left even in the destructive scene, but they stayed closer to the door. I stood there, marveling at it all, just as that beautiful moment was torn apart by another misery.

Suddenly, we heard what sounded like a twirling tornado – like a propeller whipping through the air. That sound intertwined with another one, then another. We all looked into the sky as the noise got louder, and my heart started pumping harder. There was no time to do anything. The noises were getting stronger and closer. The wind picked up as we heard the carving sounds of grenades in the ground. There were three loud booms right in front of us. Boom, boom, boom, the echoes of the sounds were deafening. Those were the propellers from the grenades that fell, one after the other, right in front of us.

The noise deafened me. Dirt and concrete flew everywhere and so did I, flying through the air again in slow motion. I thought that I was finally dead. The end of my journey had arrived. I couldn't hear or see anything but dirt and ashes flying in the air. I just felt the denotation that was making the ground shake. I looked out on the side I fell, and all I saw were ruins filled with more grenade holes, the playground wholly destroyed and everything gray. The sky was smoky and smelled like burnt concrete and death. I knew I was alive, but I could not feel my body, so I did not know if I was injured.

Boris's house was still intact, but full of grenade holes. My first thought was to run there, but I did not see my Mom, Dad, or anybody. That was the worst feeling in the world, being alone and not knowing what was happening. As my hearing came back, I heard gunshots and grenades in the distance and also cries and screams. Those screams at least gave me a sense of relief that somebody else was alive. Then I saw Dad's face. He picked me up in a panic and started running toward Boris's basement. I dug my head into his chest, crying uncontrollably. As we came into the cellar, all I could hear was the screams of my mom. I picked my head up to see her running toward me. I was so happy to see them both. She held me as Dad checked me for injuries. Then he said he was going back out to gather the rest of the people. Mom had some scratches from the fall but seemed all right. Daniel and Senka ran toward me, and they looked uninjured. Daniel had a bloody nose, scratches on his face, and his clothes were full of holes, but he seemed okay. Senka was pale, but she was walking and only had some blood on her arms. Luka was there with his mom, and they seemed okay. He was still gray, but I saw his eyes open, and that gave me some relief.

Boris and his wife were missing, as well as Luka's dad. I looked at my body again, and I could not believe that I was not dead. That was another moment in which I knew that God was there for my parents and me. Something higher was protecting us. I could not believe that we survived that. I was in shock. Mom was holding me and crying. I was in tears and worried about Dad coming back. Boris's wife came in limping, her legs bleeding as Vedad carried her. She seemed like she was passing out. We all screamed in panic when we saw her. Luka's dad seemed okay, but covered in blood, we were all unsure if it was his or Boris's wife.

The sight of so much blood made me want to vomit, but I was anxious to see my dad behind them. We ran to them to help, but Mom told me to sit next to Daniel and not touch anything. I went to Daniel, and he hugged me. He said the scratches were minor and his mom had already put alcohol on them. I told him that I was fine and asked him what had happened. He told me that he heard my Dad say the Serbian soldiers must have called in our coordinates when they saw civilians. The Fifth Brigade, a private secret sect of soldiers, had tried to destroy us. He explained that there were always sleazy spies in the army, even the TO army, that are like traitors. They're hidden soldiers, posing as civilians. I looked at him, and he knew how my mind was racing. He smiled, "No, none of us." I was so scared and confused. We could have died out there.

I just hugged Daniel tighter; then we heard cries from Boris's wife. Grenade shrapnel had torn her up. As I bent my neck to try and see her how bad she was, finally Dad came in. He was carrying an unconscious Boris on his back. He was covered in dark red blood and gushing more of it, as well as black gore from a deep wound. Daniel and I gagged at the sight of him; we broke in a cold sweat. We all thought Boris was dead. Mom screamed, and Senka passed out on the floor. He looked like a corpse already. Dad put him down, and everyone attended to him. His body was gray, his eyes sunken and red. The wound was a big hole right above his heart. I felt weak and shaky. I was looking at a dead man. My dad was trying to cover the wound as best as he could, but I knew that it was too late. His eyes were wide and staring, empty like his soul had left his body already. There was nothing we could do — especially when, in the next moment, we were all bathed in a flash of white light.

The next thing I knew, I woke up in Mom's arms. I was queasy and asked

Mom what had happened. She tearfully told me that grenades hit us, and it had been horrible. I asked Dad where Boris was, and he said to me that he was not doing well. The truck picked him up. I burst into tears because I knew what it meant to be picked up by the death truck. Boris's wife was sleeping. She was scratched up. I could only imagine how she felt. Dad kissed me on my forehead and said that God saved me, "Boris was right in front of you when the grenades fell." The grenade shrapnel would have finished right in my head and killed me on the spot, but instead, it landed in Boris's shoulder. He kissed me again and said, "You are meant to grow old and do something wonderful with your life." Tears rolled down my face. I had an instant flash of what had happened, remembering the grenade's noise and Boris's body in front of me. I was so sad that he took that shrapnel instead of me, but I thanked God all the same. Dad kept hugging me, even with blood crusted all over him. Mom kissed me, and I lay back on her, hugging her close and telling her I loved her.

Later that day, Boris's wife woke up in screams. Everyone tried to comfort her. I could not imagine the emotional pain she was going through — another death among us. I looked at Senka, and she was quiet. She scared me the most. I knew that she was gone by the way that she didn't respond to the screams. That night, all I could dream of was Boris. I hoped he was in a better place. I hoped that his wife was okay and that we all made it out of there. I did not want to wake up and face this reality anymore. I didn't want to face Boris's wife or this danger anymore. We had all looked death in the eye and tasted the wrath of those grenades. The room was constricting and smelled of death, destruction, and blood. We were cooped up with no water or food and death all around us. As those thoughts rushed through my head, I thought I was going crazy. I opened my eyes and hugged Mom and Dad tight, needing support and clinging to sanity. Luka was crying, and I worried that we were going to lose him because he looked even

---

worse. I couldn't bear this anymore. I couldn't take it. I wanted it to stop. I wanted to die, death would be easier.

The next morning was very gray, both literally and figuratively. The mood in the room was awful; Boris's wife was in the corner crying and not talking to anyone. Senka was speechless as usual, holding onto Daniel, who was quiet too. He was not himself at all. Little Luka was just as silent. even my parents seemed to be in another world. I wanted to go back to sleep and not live through all of this. We lost somebody else, and we each knew that we were next. We were all slowly losing our minds.

Dad told me that he had decided that we needed to get out of here if we had any chance at survival. He had been communicating with TO and his best friend's family that lives in Dobrinja, a neighborhood ten miles from the airport. That neighborhood had suffered enormous damage from heavy artillery, but it also was a lot bigger and had a big base with food and water. His friend's family would take care of us there. I asked Dad how we'd get there, and he just mumbled, "I'm still working on that." I wondered about the others, but he said that it would only be us three. They would have to find another way. It tortured him, but he could not find a way to help others and save his own family at the same time. I asked him when we were leaving, and he just said, "Soon."

The night brought with it the sounds of grenades and bazookas. The darkness brought more of that danger and uncertainty we were so eager to escape. Nothing, however, confirmed the feeling of urgency to leave more than what happened on the night of September 23, 1992. A night of horror.

Chapter Ten

We all sat in the basement, as usual, counting the minutes of horror, remembering the lost souls. The artillery was unusually heavy that night. Grenades landed closer than ever. The gunshots sounded different. The candle flickered at each shake and detonations, especially when a colossal grenade detonated right next door. Everything seemed closer and bigger, making us all uneasy, but we got even more nervous when Dad jumped up and ran to the door. It was as if he knew that trouble was right outside of the door. He whispered to Mom, "Guerilla troops are roaming the neighborhood. We've never heard that many gunshots and rifles this close. It can only mean Serbian soldiers were cleansing the houses." That was our worst nightmare come true. They would enter, kill all the men, and torture us women and children before taking us to concentration camps. I started shaking, and Mom took Senka's hand and started to pray. We heard another considerable explosion coming from a tank right outside. God knows what they were destroying, but it was too close for comfort. My heart pounded. Daniel came close, in tears. Dad and Vedad paced by the door in a panic.

The gunshots got louder, and so did our prayers, hoping that God would save us. We knew that evil was coming. We were helpless, worried, terrified, and ready to pass out. Only a miracle could save us. It was the worst feeling to know that rape, torture, and death was so near, and there was nothing that we could do. All of a sudden, we heard men's voices outside the door. Dad lifted his rifle and signaled for us to cover up in the corner. There were more gunshots right outside as the voices came to the door. My breath stopped, and a strange silence overcame the place – except for the murmur of prayers – broken by a soldier outside yelling, " Open the door, pigs! Or we will bring it down!"

Mom pressed her hand over my mouth to silence my sobs. I was hyperventilating as Mom covered me. The soldier yelled again, "Open the door, or we'll shoot." That moment burned into my memory. I struggled for breath as Mom squeezed me, praying to God to save us. Then, out of nowhere, we heard another explosion and flames roaring, followed by gunshots. I closed my eyes and waited for torture. The fear and anxiety were beyond this earth. It seemed like an hour of carnage passed by, but it was just a few seconds. Afterward, I lifted my head and looked around. We were all still there; the door stayed closed, and nobody came in.

I was confused, "What happened?" Dad went to the door. We pleaded with him to stay put, but he didn't listen. He tried to look through the side cracks of the door. We didn't hear anything coming from outside at all anymore, no voices or gunshots, just the residual sound of flame. "We were saved. Someone must have distracted them." He had a relieved look on his face. He wanted to go out to investigate, but we pulled him back, just in case. We were all relieved, stunned, and confused. Mom was still hugging me, and Daniel was in Senka's arms. I will never forget her face. For the first time, I saw relief in her eyes and a glimpse of hope. She smiled, knowing that we were saved, "God saved us. It was a miracle. God saved us from the torture." A sense of warmth came over me. She was right. Something saved us — a miracle. We were supposed to have died, but we were still here.

I'll never forget that moment; it was the kind of miracle that people tell their children. It made me a true believer. In that instant, I knew God would take care of us. I was blessed by positivity in that bad situation. We were all in shock. I ran to Dad and hugged him, "Honey, we are going to be okay." I asked what had happened, why they had left, "It must have been the TO that shot at them. They scared them away. That's the only thing it could be. Go sit down and try to sleep."

I sat with Mom and Daniel as Dad told everyone, "We are safe, but we can't sit here and wait. We have to move out." It was scary but true. The soldiers would be back again, and we needed to getaway. I sat surrounded by Mom's arms, waiting to see what we were going to do. Still, in shock and amazement, I could only think of what Dad had told me: *that I was meant to do something in this life.* That was the strength and inspiration that kept going through my mind. Those were the small things that kept us sane. The moments that gave us hope. Our survival instincts kicked in, and we wanted to escape and live life. We would fight for our lives.

We wanted to survive and were now willing to do anything to get out. We had grown from terrified and lost, almost dying, to inspired and rushed with adrenaline. None of us slept that night. We were all too eager to see what would happen next. Dad went out to assess our escape and communicate with TO and see what they could do for us. I trusted Dad as any 10-year-old would. He was my hero. He would find a way to get us out. He said he would go at night when it was less obvious and he would have more cover.

I dozed off in Mom's arms, exhausted. Dad held Mom as she laid on him and caressed my face. They were discussing an escape plan. Dad had an idea that would require TO's help. As he was trying to explain, Boris's wife started talking to herself in a low voice and swaying back and forth in her seat. We couldn't understand what she was saying, but her body language was aggressive. When we looked over, she seemed to stop. We knew she was uneasy but didn't think anything of it and continued our conversation. Then, out of nowhere, she stood up in rage. Tears were rolling down her face as she bolted toward the door, so quickly that none of us had time to react.

76

She unlocked the door quickly and opened it, yelling, "You Chetniks! You fucking murderers! Come get me, you pigs! Come get me!" A cold sweat came over everybody, and my heart fell to the floor. She ran out so quickly. Vedad ran after her, and Dad bolted out too but took him a bit because we were both on top of him. They tried their best to get to her before she went outside, but it was too late. She was out in the street, in the middle of the day, with high activity out there and no chance. We could hear her in the street, yelling. Then, in a matter of seconds, shots were fired. All we heard was two sniper shots, short and sharp. Boris's wife was gone.

Vedad and Dad came in and closed the door. It all happened so quickly. I guess her sorrow was too intense. She didn't see a way out. She was alone, and they had killed her husband. She lost it. We all just covered our mouths and fell to the floor. Mom was in shock. We all lost our breath. It was unbelievable. I didn't know if I had dreamt all of that. I looked around, one more time, and everyone was there, except Boris's wife.

Dad looked at me, "Honey, you fell asleep for a long time. Are you okay?" I said I was, and asked what had happened. He only answered, "We lost another soul." I hadn't dreamt it at all. She was gone. She went crazy and committed suicide. I felt horrible. We were all going mad. I felt helpless and consumed with sorrow until Dad lifted my head, "I spoke to TO. They will help us get out." As much as I wanted to tell him that he should never go out there again, I knew that staying here was a death sentence. The news lifted my mood, even if everyone in that room was on the edge of falling.

Daniel and Senka came over and said they would stick to any plan my father had in mind. Dad said that everyone would be on their own, leaving at different times, so as not to make us into a big target. He went out that night, to follow the TO hiding spots and tunnels and finalize a plan of escape. Dad said the

TO soldiers were the ones that blew up the tank across the street. The tank was where the Serbian soldiers came from that were knocking on the door. They were going to break in and kill us all. They had been guerilla cleaning the neighborhood. The TO had told Dad that the spies knew that we were in here and they came for us. Goosebumps covered my body when I heard that. The TO soldiers had known that we were here. They had arrived just in time. They were the miracle that saved us, and he had thanked them. We all knew that we needed to get out. Dad went over the plan of escape. I turned to my mom and hugged her, and her heart was beating hard. She was nervous but holding me with confidence. The escape plan had consumed our minds so much that we had forgotten about Boris's wife. Or, as terrible as it sounds, we were getting used to death. My only prayer was that now she was peacefully back with her husband.

Late that night, I asked Mom what we were going to do, "Baby, we will escape on our own to Dobrinja. We will leave tomorrow, very early, when the things are calmer, and the soldiers are not shooting every minute." I was glad to hear that, but, my instincts of flight or fight raised my adrenaline. I was nervous. The plan meant going out there and exposing ourselves to being shot. It was scary, nerve-racking, and surreal. We were risking our lives again. Dad wrapped his arms around us, "Honey, everything will be fine. We will escape. I promise." He told me all of the details of the plan. We would travel in a Yugo that a TO member was putting outside in the morning. We would use tunnels and drive on a specific road at a particular time while the TO tried to hold fire and protect us. We would need to be fast. Dobrinja was about 15 miles away and our friends, Ana and Ivan, were waiting for us there. The TO was going to help us within their base.

The plan seemed simple, but I was so scared I couldn't concentrate. All I could think of was that we would be out there, and it could be the last time we saw the light. The chance that we could die was very high, but my heart couldn't

78

accept that. Human survival instincts kick in, even at that young age. I was scared to go, scared to die, but I dared to do it. Dad continued trying to calm me, "Honey, we will escape. Nothing will happen to us. Do you trust me? I will get us out." There was that confidence, and that assurance again. Dad was amazing at motivating everyone, and he made me feel better like we had no other choice but to try and succeed. We couldn't stay here anymore. I remember feeling dizzy and in a weak haze. None of us had enough food or water, and we were all on an adrenaline high. We were nervous and tired, and we needed to get some more food and escape this hell.

That night was a special one: the last time I ever spent with Daniel, Senka and everyone else. It was bittersweet. I didn't know where Daniel was going to end up, or if I was ever going to see him again. I told him, "You are my best friend, and you will always be in my heart." We hugged and cried on each other – everybody in that basement did – for what seemed like the entire night. We were telling each other that it would be okay, and we would see each other again. Luka and his family were together, still holding on, even if they looked gray. My heart hurt for little Luka, but he was still alive and fighting, and he had his father next to him, injured or not.

My heart was breaking, knowing that we would be separated. I wanted Daniel and Senka to come with us and asked Dad to consider it. He was very stern and said that the TO was barely taking us there, and he had to try to save us first. TO did promise my dad to help others escape as well. I felt so guilty about leaving them there, but there was nothing I could do. I prayed that TO would help them, and I prayed that would see them again. Daniel was trying to be brave, telling me that they would find a way to survive. They just needed to get out of there. He promised me that we would see each other again. All of us stayed awake for most of the night, which did not feel as long as the others. We listened to grenades fall and rifles fire – still afraid that the soldiers would come for us. However, that night, we were filled with love and community. We talked and encouraged each other.

I didn't let Daniel out of my arms, and Mom and Senka were holding each other and praying. Our minds and souls were getting ready for the next chapter of our lives; preparing to escape and letting our friends know that they would always be in our hearts. It is funny how, even in the worst situations, we find something to remember that is beautiful and real. The early morning came, and I remember hugging Daniel, crying, and telling him that he was my best friend. Those people will always be in my heart. My memories will always be filled with beautiful thoughts when it comes to them. That was the last time I ever saw any of them. The last time I saw Daniel.

Chapter Eleven

Very early that morning, while there was still fog outside and it was barely light, we saw the red Yugo in the street. It was delivered a few minutes earlier by the TO connection. My heart pumped hard. Dad yelled for us to hurry up and get in. All we had with us was a little bag with three shirts and our passports. My adrenaline was high, and all I could think of was escaping, surviving. As we ran to the car, the streets seemed so gray and sad. There wasn't a soul on the streets, not even a cat or a dog or even a rat. The fog covered most of the area, and it was hard to see in the distance, which was a good thing while we tried to stay as invisible as possible. The fog was again one of the miracles that contributed to protecting us in our escape. It felt like a horror movie: nobody on the streets, deserted, dead. We got in the car and Dad started driving. He took the back road through the dug out channels out of the neighborhood. The dirt road right after the last few remaining houses leading out of the community.

We drove past burnt-out houses, big holes and bullet scars everywhere, cars, and buildings with chunks missing, and the rebar hanging out. The worst was the smell of burnt concrete, of fire and burning flesh. Dad was driving like a maniac, going as fast as the little Yugo could. It was terrifying. We couldn't see anything in front of us because of the fog, and the car revved and struggled the entire drive, but *we kept going*. I held tight to Mom, and she squeezed me even closer. I could feel her heart beating so fast like it was going to come out of her chest.

At some point, I stopped being able to recognize where we were. Buildings were missing, no trees at all, and barricades everywhere. My neighborhood looked like one of those Mad Max movies, where there were only fires, destruction, chaos, and death. It wasn't a movie, though, it was real. I was living in it. I didn't recognize the way because the TO had excavated a different route under their control. It was like a new ditch with a secret road. I tried to keep my head buried in Mom's arms and not look outside. Tears streamed from my eyes, but I didn't feel like I was crying. It's hard to explain the jumble of emotions. I was scared, sad, pumped, invincible, nervous, hungry, and dizzy all at the same time.

The jerking of the car going over the new dirt road forced me to look out and see what was happening. At that point, the visibility got a tad bit better just around us, so it was easier to see, but the fog was still dense to see in the distance. At that point, as we rocked side to side, I wish I didn't look. Mom covered my head quickly, but I had enough time to see the horror. There were piles of dead bodies on the side of the road, right next to us, rotting away. Blood everywhere, bodies discombobulated, arms hanging, and the most disgusting stench I have ever smelled in my life. Mom screamed and held me down in her lap. I could not believe what I saw. I couldn't help thinking that there could be somebody we knew in there. The bodies were covered in crusted blood looking tortured. I got nauseous, so sick to my stomach that I didn't think I could keep it in.

Mom tried to calm me down, grabbing me hard, "Listen to me, baby. They are in a better place. Their souls are happy. Don't focus on their bodies. Remember what Njanja always said: 'When I die throw me in the river, but I will be happy.'" Even as horrible as I felt, that made me feel better because I thought of my Njanja, my grandma, and how strong she was. Mom held me tight. I was shaken up, but at least not hysterical. I was trying to focus on getting out, instead of the chaos I was seeing.

Those people didn't deserve to die. Fear and cold sweat ran over my body. I started shivering. Dad didn't say a word. He was concentrating on driving and getting us out of there. When we passed the bodies, he put out his hand and shoved my head down into Mom's lap. He kept driving, and we kept bouncing. It was hard to stay still in the car, and I worried it wouldn't make it through.

I'm not sure how long we drove, but it seemed like forever. Finally, we came to a stop. I picked up my head a little bit and saw TO soldiers in front of us, wearing green berets. They were friendly with my dad. I knew my dad negotiated with them, and negotiations still worked at this point. These were people from the neighborhood that my dad knew, mostly Muslim, which confused me. Why were they friendly with my dad? It was nice to think that there was still some humanity left. I was still shivering and crying, scared to the bone. My heart was in my chest. The soldiers talked to Dad, telling him where he needed to go and warning him that we would now be out in the open, out of the TO's territory, the no man land and an open target to snipers and grenades. However, they told him what road would be best to reach TO in Dobrinja.

My father gave them something in return but, to this day, I don't know what it was. I've always assumed it was money but, whatever it was, this was war. We had to do anything to survive. They moved a big truck out of the way, their barricade, and we proceeded to drive into another ditch. This one was even bouncier and rockier. I was lost, with no idea where we were. Mom's hands were cold and shivering, and her fear made me even more nervous. I clenched my teeth and curled up as she held me tighter, "I love you, honey. Everything will be okay." As much as my survival instincts wanted to believe her, I was nervous. I was scared that we were going to die in this car. At least we would be together, I thought. At least I was with my parents. I didn't want to think that way, but it did make me feel better. I just wanted to get out and be safe. I wanted to survive.

We kept driving and, all of a sudden, we were on a smooth, regular road — a highway out of our neighborhood on the way to Dobrinja, the one road we took to go in and out. Dad was going so fast that I worried we would crash, but Dad was an excellent driver and handled the Yugo just fine.

There were detonations in the distance as we drove on the deserted road. The open space scared me. That cold sweat came over me again. I was terrified, but I knew that Dobrinja was not that far from this point from my memory. That was the only thing keeping all of us sane. We traveled only a few kilometers, but it seemed like we were crossing the ocean. We were going as fast as we could, and even with the fog red Yugo was a perfect target. All of a sudden, we heard shots. The detonations were so close. Not sure if they were aimed at us or not but either way, our hearts stopped. Dad swerved out of fear and just in case. Mom and I started screaming, thinking we were going to die right then. I was horrified. Dad shouted for us to keep our heads down in our seats. I was in shock, breathing so hard that I started choking. Dad kept swerving, driving as fast as he could. I was sure we were going to die, if not by the shots then by crashing.

We heard shots all around us, but none hit us. All I could see was the floor of the car. I closed my eyes and Mom, and I prayed — all of a sudden, a harsh detonation that we swayed side to side so harshly. The hard jerks did not stop Dad or turn us over. It helped that he was a professional racecar driver back in the day. He maintained control by a miracle, but he was cursing, "We're almost there, stay low." Mom covered me. I smelled smoke and burning rubber, the tires were working hard, and they were smoking. All I could hear was my heavy breathing and shots outside. I was bouncing all over the place and trying to hold on to Mom, "Hold on. We are almost there, hold on." I focused on his voice like a ray of sunshine. It was what kept me going.

Then, finally, I didn't hear the shots as much, or as intensely as I did before. We were going into a building. A shadow fell over us, and it was getting darker. I felt the car slow down. We were there and still alive. I heard a man's voice saying to park. In my heart, I felt tremendous relief. I heard Dad talking to them. We were in Dobrinja. I held my head up and saw an underground tunnel and a couple of TO soldiers, in green uniforms and berets. We were safe. Mom helped me out of the car, which was still smoking from burning tires.

The burning car smell was strong, but the tunnel smelled even worse. It was so dark and eerie. It looked like a set from a sci-fi movie. I was terrified but relieved that we made it inside. The soldiers were intimidating. They didn't say much and were very military-like. Once we got out of the car, the other soldiers took it back outside. We were immediately escorted into the building with a soldier and Dad leading us. I took Mom's hand, put my head down, and just walked. I couldn't believe that we had made it here alive.

All of a sudden, we heard our names called — it was Ana and Ivan, my parent's close friends who lived there and who were helping us escape. My parents ran to them, and we all hugged. They were happy to see us and made me feel better, safer. We were going to stay there for a few days, and then Ana's connections were planning to get us out of Sarajevo with the soldier's help. They had one son, Igor, who was two years older than me. They took us to their apartment. Ana was of Catholic descent, but Ivan was Muslim. That's why TO was allowing them to stay in their base. Ivan was also useful to TO because he was a sniper in the army. That's how Dad knew him. They served together in the military and were terrific friends.

Their apartment was on the fifth floor; wood covered the windows, and mattresses were everywhere. It was dark and muggy but felt safe. They had oil lamps, and all slept in the living room. Ana told us where we were going to sleep and said they had some bread and water and smoked meat for us. My heart jumped when she said she had food. The last time I had eaten was the day before, and that had been flour and water. Even though they had more food than us, they also looked like skeletons. I guess everyone's appearance changed under that physical and emotional struggle. All of us had gotten more scared and depressed, being in a war under the everyday fear of dying. Ana and Ivan told us to have a seat and talk.

They sent us kids into the other room to play. "*Play?*" I thought to myself. The last thing I wanted to do was play. I wanted to survive and be part of the plan. Igor also thought the same thing. He wanted to take a gun and be part of the action, a typical teenage boy. We stood by the door and listened to the grown-ups. I overheard them, telling Dad not to say his name. The TO here could not know that he was Serbian. They had to use Mom's maiden name and make one up for Dad. The TO here did not tolerate Serbs. Many soldiers had lost family members to Serbian grenades and shots. Dad looked critical, mumbling, "They didn't get to you too? You know what I am. You've been my best friend for twenty years." Ivan hugged him and whispered something. I guess this war had everyone brainwashed and crazy; people forgot who they were and who their friends were.

I asked Igor how everything was here, what was happening, and if they have to go to the basement. Igor told me that here they were protected, because it is a TO base and they have guns and weapons, "They try to protect this territory. Serbians will not take it. We get hit by grenades and shots, but we protect ourselves from those pigs. TO supplies us with food and water and Dad goes out there and shoots them. We need to protect our town. I wish I were there with them, shooting at them." My stomach was turning, listening to how different the atmosphere was here. Only persons on their side mattered. I couldn't help but think of all the many decent people who were Serbian. I was scared and uncomfortable. Igor was nothing like Daniel, the best friend I didn't know I would never see again.

Igor didn't know what to do with me, so I just left the room and went to where my parents were. Mom got up immediately and hugged me, asking what was wrong. Igor insisted that he didn't do anything. I told her that I was fine, just scared. Ana got some bread and water for us. We started to eat, and Ivan explained that, at one point in our escape, the Serbian army would meet us and we would have to make sure not to say Mom's name. We were to use her Serbian one. It was Ana's work connections that were helping us. They got money in exchange.

They spoke more of our route and the details of what we were to say and do. I lost them after a few minutes because I was exhausted. Even though it was the middle of the day, my body and mind had been through such trauma. We almost died that day in the car. I am not sure how we survived at all, and did not get hit in the middle of an empty road. I replayed the drive in my head over and over, adrenaline pumping in my heart. We were saved again, with no other explanation than it was another miracle.

I woke that night next to my parents on the mattress in the living room. I had been dreaming about our car escape. I was confused for a minute, and then I remembered where we were. The sound of grenades woke me up. They were shaking the whole building, and I heard shots. It seemed close, but for some reason, they didn't sound as dangerous as they did in our old neighborhood. This complex was more significant and more secluded, so the grenades and gunfire were not as loud. It was strange to admit, but I needed that intense, loud sound now. It almost comforted me. The sounds of grenades were my lullabies.

Chapter Twelve

When I woke the next morning, a little light was coming through the cracks in the wood behind the mattress. Dad was already talking with Ivan, and Ana was with Mom. I got up and ran to her, "What's wrong, Mom?" She quickly composed herself, "Nothing, baby. It's okay. I was telling her that I missed her and that I'm happy we are alive." She told me not to worry about a thing, and that Ana was coming with us. I was nervous and uncomfortable. I felt so awful and out of place. I was ready to leave. Dad hugged me good morning and told us that we would go in a day or so. They were finalizing plans. Ana had spoken to her connections and assured us that we would be fine if we just stuck to the route and strategy.

I was scared, but I needed to believe in the escape plan and my parents. Ana gave us a piece of bread and some water. I noticed that it was getting hot in the apartment. No air was coming in the shuttered windows. Igor came out and said that he talked to TO. Ivan started yelling at him, "What in the world were you doing talking to the soldiers!?!" Ivan was mad, and he had told Igor not to talk to anybody. I wanted to know what was going on. Were we safe here? Were these soldiers the good ones? What exactly was down there in their basement base? I asked Igor what had happened. He said that TO had captured a couple of Serbian soldiers and that they were torturing them. They said they were forming another base and would need more people to fight.

Igor was thinking of joining. I looked at him and thought to myself that he was going to get himself killed. He said that TO knows the Serbian army was closing in. They were coming down from the mountains with heavy artillery. They were getting more dangerous, and they needed to fight back harder. I could tell that the situation there was only getting worse. We needed to get out soon. I knew that this city was soon to become "Code Zero." My heart pounded with fear, thinking about our impossible task. How in the world were we going to be able to get out? How would my Muslim mother pass all of those Serbian soldiers? I was too young to analyze everything, but I focused on the basics. My survival instinct made me think about how the TO soldiers were not innocent either. Each side was guilty of terrible things in this dirty war. We were no longer in a peaceful Sarajevo. There were hard lines between Serbs, Muslims, and Croats, and those lines were getting harder as the war went on. Brothers were killing each other.

My thoughts were interrupted by a commotion from the hallway. We got up and ran to the door, where Ivan and Ana were talking to soldiers. We overheard them saying that they would not tolerate having "an enemy" here. He meant my family and me. He was telling Ivan that we needed to leave. Ivan tried to assure him that we were not enemies, but they just barked, "The Serb better leave soon. We don't trust him." They were talking about Dad, the only Serb that was here.

We were enemies to them. It was so frustrating. They did not even know Dad, or who he was. He was married to a Muslim, and he didn't consider himself a Serb at all. He was a good man who helped everyone, and the TO in our neighborhood helped him. I wanted to shout that at them. It was so unfair, and horrible to feel unjustly like an outsider. Mom came over to me quickly and covered my face. The soldiers said something else that I could not hear, and they left after Ivan slammed the door as hard as he could. Ivan gave my dad a sad look, "It's okay. We will leave tomorrow morning. Have Ana arrange with the soldiers." Ivan was not happy, but he needed to protect his family and, to do that, he needed us to leave. The atmosphere was horrible and accurately reflected the tragedy of this war. Brothers and best friends couldn't rely on each other anymore. The problem was too deeply rooted. Our city, our state, and our country were all going to hell.

Mom held me and comforted me as much as she could, but she didn't have anything to say. I was confused, hurt, and just felt horrible. As much as I wanted to leave, I was scared of coming close to death again. All I could think of was that Dad was a good guy. Why couldn't they see that? The day went on in agonized suspense. Ana set up the connection on the Serbian side of Dobrinja's midpoint. The soldiers would wait for us there in a tank, and then take us out to the Serbian base in the mountains. My heart stopped. *The mountains?* She quickly told us that they would export us out of Bosnia there. "They were paid very well," she said, "And they are answering to my connections in Serbia." We would get from here, to the Serbian side using a tunnel. Neither faction wanted to have any contact with the other. The tunnel would lead us to the outside street on the other edge of Dobrinja. From there, we just needed to walk to the soldiers who would be waiting for us. The signal would be smoke coming from a tank. Ana spoke in detail about what we needed to do, and Mom was paying attention very carefully.

Ana reminded us that, once we got to the Serbian side of the city, Mom must not mention that her name was Muslim. She needed to make up a Serbian name. Serbians wanted to save the so-called Serbian families from the Muslim and Croat bases. The war was new, so that kind of diplomacy still existed. Negotiations and money worked very well. I was overwhelmed by it all, but I knew my parents would be able to follow directions, and I would be right in between them. All I felt was my heart beating. I was scared, but I was ready. I guess when you are a young child, everything can transform into a new adventure in your head. I was ready, but I was still terrified. All I could think of was having an "ordinary" life again. Hope was my fuel.

Lost in thought, I saw Dad walk toward the other room. I wasn't sure why he was not talking to Ana. I got up, followed him, and asked him what was wrong. He and Mom both came close to me and sat me down. Dad started talking, and I will never forget those words, "Honey, Daddy can't come with you and Mom. Men are not allowed to leave." My heart stopped as Dad continued, "Baby, I will get out later, and we will see each other again. I promise. But now you have to go with Mom. It's the only way to keep you safe." My world crumbled. All I did was cry. I felt a massive weight on my chest, and I felt as I was losing air. A part of me died that night, and that part attached to the feeling of abandonment. I was hysterical, screaming, "No! No, I am not leaving without you. We are all going together." I turned to my mom, "Make him go. We can find a way for all of us to go, please!"

Dad hugged me. That was one of the few times I ever saw him cry. Mom was crying hysterically too. We were all hugging and holding on tight. I kept telling him, "Dad, what will you do? How are we going to meet up? Am I ever going to see you again? I don't want to leave without you. What are we going to do without you?" Dad kept saying, "Everything will be okay. We need to work through things. You will be safe with mom in Serbia. There will be people there to help you, and you will be fine. I will stay with the neighbors in our neighborhood and see what we can hold down. I made some good friends there." I couldn't stop crying. I was so scared that I would never see him again. I could not take it, and all Dad could do was hold me and look closely into my eyes, "Baby, I promise I will see you again. You trust me, don't you?" His confident stare always worked. It calmed me a little, but I was still hysterical. I held him tight and didn't let go. Mom held me from the other side, as he kept whispering, "Baby, it will be okay. I will see you again. You need to be safe and get out. That is the most important thing ever. This is the only way, honey."

I kept crying and holding onto him like never before in my life. I could not believe dad was staying behind. I was devastated. Ana came in and told me that everything would be okay. Ivan would be waiting too. Nothing anybody said would make me feel better. I wanted my dad with me. I couldn't imagine life without him. I was scared for him, going back to that hell. I was afraid for him to stay. I felt guilty that we were going to go and leave him behind, "We will stay with you. We can survive here with you." Dad held me tight and reminded me that I was meant to do something in my life, that I deserved a normal one. That's what parents have to do for their children. "It will be okay, honey. I promise. I love you." I continued crying. My heart broke.

The next thing I remember was hearing grenade blasts close to us. The walls were shaking, and the wood was almost coming off of the windows. Tonight, the danger was closer. We had to go to the basement. I was so devastated that I was going to leave my dad. I didn't want to let go of him. I held him tight. I needed to make sure I spent every minute with him. Mom wept with me. I know she was trying to be strong, but she could not hide how difficult this was for her. I couldn't take it. I was whispering, "Please go with us, Daddy." He held me and kept saying, "Shhhh, I promise we will be okay, and we will be together again." I knew that was the final decision. We just needed to do it and pray that Dad could keep the promise. I had to think that way. I didn't have any other options. Hope was the only thing left to help keep my sanity.

Dad carried me down to the basement, and Mom was next to us, holding my hand and Dad's shoulder at the same time. The grenades were vicious, and they were close. All I could think of was my dad and leaving him tomorrow. I was used to the grenades, even the close ones. I accepted the dangers and didn't pay attention until the detonations were strong enough to knock us off our feet. The night continued with shots and grenades pounding away, but what was scarier were the looks we got in the basement. Each section had a basement for every couple of apartments, and we shared this with some neighbors. Everyone was quiet. In the shadows of candles, we all sat down on the floor and listened to the grenades.

I didn't want to feel that feeling of unwelcome, but it was there. The tension was there. The grenades were active, but I didn't care about anything but being with my parents. I held Dad tight, and Mom was on the other side, holding him even tighter. He was kissing both of us on the forehead and caressing us. I was numb and utterly heartbroken. I was so worried about him that I didn't care if we all stayed and died together. Every time I tried to say something, both of my parents would silence me and reassure me that they had a plan. I was so exhausted. All I wanted to do was hold my dad and, spend every last minute with him, but I couldn't keep my eyes open. That was the last night and the last time I spent with my dad in Sarajevo.

Chapter Thirteen

The next morning, we were back in the apartment. It was still early and dark. My parents had brought me up, and I woke because they were talking and crying. Mom was hugging and kissing Dad and telling him how much she loved him. He was holding her and trying to calm her down. He said to her that we would be together again. That he loved her very much and to be tough and take care of me. They would communicate with military phones when he could. They were saying their goodbyes, and I felt a knot in my stomach. I wanted to throw up. I couldn't believe this was the day we were leaving, going through terrible danger again and, this time, without Dad. I looked over to Ana and Igor and Ivan, all saying goodbye as well. It was very emotional; we were leaving our dads behind. My dad came over to me and wiped off his tears and hugged me. I remember bawling out loud and holding him tight. It was hard to see him like that. I was so worried about him. I hoped he knew what he was doing. I was going to miss him so much. I hugged him and told him how much I loved him, and he told me, "Baby, I love you. I will always be there with you. I promise we will meet again. Please be strong for your mom and help her and take care of each other." I couldn't say anything more. I just hugged him and held him, while the tears ran down my face.

Ana and Igor came over and said that it was time. The TO soldiers were at the door, waiting to escort us. Ivan and Dad went with us to lead us through the tunnel. I was holding Dad and Mom's hands on either side, with Ana and Igor and Ivan in front of us. Mom only had one bookbag with us, with some changes of clothes, money, paperwork, and bread – that was all we took with us. I got scared as we approached the tunnel and squeezed Dad's hand hard. He just kept smiling at me and saying, "Don't worry, baby. It will be okay." He was not very convincing this time, because I think he was worried about trusting these people getting us out. I can see, now, how truly hard – if not insane and suicidal – that must have been. Back then, however, the only thing going through my mind was that I would not have my Dad.

As the tunnel got closer, my adrenaline was pumping. I wanted to survive and get out. That childish excitement was there again, there to help me face the danger. I kept holding on to Dad and Mom as we were walking. Ana kept assuring us that we would be okay with the soldiers and that they wanted to get innocent women and children out. That helped a little, and explained why men couldn't go. They wanted men to stay and fight.

We started walking through TO territory, a Muslim tunnel that was dug out and would eventually exit into no man's land, which would connect to the Serbian area. This part was also supposedly protecting women and children. While we were in the Serbian territory, we would walk in the middle of the street to reach our transportation. I was going over these plans in my head over and over. I could see the sun at the end of the tunnel. I started shaking. I could not believe that I was about to leave my dad there. I hugged him super tight, while tears poured out, "Honey. Concentrate. I love you. Go." Mom hugged him, gave him a huge kiss, and told him she loved him. Ana and her family did the same until a soldier looked at his watch and said it was time. I looked at Dad one more time and read his lips as he mouthed to me, "I promise."

That was the promise I held on to so tight, that was my new found hope and Bible. Mom took my hand, and we left, behind Igor and Ana, who told us, "Follow me exactly and do what I do. Go slowly and, when I tell you to put your hands up, do it." Ana was a strong woman, brave, and confident. I admired her. She led us out of that scary tunnel, into the light. I turned and looked at Dad. I saw his eyes watering. Mom gave him a look of love and then held me tight as we went forward into the light.

Outside, the city looked so awful. We walked down the middle of an abandoned two-way street. The tall buildings seemed to warn us of snipers inside, each one of us in their deadly view. It was dark and miserable out there. We were the only living beings on the street. The with A spooky atmosphere and gray clouds surrounded us. We knew we could die at any minute. The awful smell of destruction and look of ruins reminded me of horror movies, and yet here we were in the middle of it, real live targets. The soldiers were everywhere in the buildings around us, with rifles and the 5th brigade – the spies – who could send a grenade at any time to blow us all to pieces. It was so silent like we were the only people on the planet. The buildings were full of bullet holes and grenade-blasted scars that exposed broken rebar and shattered windows shattered. I held on to Mom, and we all got into a tighter formation. Ana kept whispering, "Keep moving. We walked for what seemed like miles until we reached our contact but, it was probably only a block or two.

All we were hoping for was for it still to be true that the soldiers wanted to make sure women and children made it out. That was the negotiation made from Ana's diplomatic work and with substantial compensation. Somewhere in the distance, the racing bullets and grenades spread a thundering sound. We continued down the street, our heads down and hands up praying, walking until we saw a smoking tank. That was our contact point. We stopped for a moment, and the tank released smoke one more time. That was our cue to come closer. I got another knot in my stomach as I saw rough-looking Serbian soldiers behind the tank with massive guns. They all had beards and long hair. I got worried. Those were the same soldiers that were destroying our neighborhood. Those were the same soldiers that were the killers in my mind.

I had no time to be scared, however, so I remembered my dad. I kept telling myself that not all Serbs were terrible. These will help us. As we kept walking, I couldn't help getting more nervous. Instead of feeling relieved to get out of the open road, I was getting more worried about coming in contact with these soldiers. It was the way they were looking at us like we were pieces of meat. Our Serbian last name was our only savior out of Sarajevo. We were Serbian women and children, regardless of the whole truth. I kept telling myself they will help us. I tightened the grip on Mom's hand when I saw two soldiers sneaking out from the behind the tank and coming toward us, signaling us to walk faster. We sped up a little. As we approached, three of them pulled machine guns on us, while the other two brutally searched every inch of our bodies. I felt so scared, and their hands were going everywhere on me. I felt their filthy hands on my private parts over and over. They didn't care about privacy, and they touched us everywhere.

   I was breathing so hard and crying. I had never felt like that in my life. It was even worse to watch them search my mom, their hands touching every part of her body. I was scared, and I was also getting mad. If only Dad were here, he would have killed them all. I was raging, but the fear kept me just crying. Thank goodness, they didn't do anything more than just search. I will never forget the terrified look on Mom's face. We had no idea what these soldiers would do. They could have raped us or violated us in any way. They were laughing, enjoying our fear, enjoying that power. I hated them for that, but I kept quiet. We all did. When they stopped, they again pointed the guns in our backs. They pushed us like animals into a little van parked behind the tank. Feeling the cold steel of the gun on my back, I felt like my heart would stop beating. They tied our hands and covered our heads with bags so that we could not see their secret way of escaping from that part of Sarajevo. I heard the van start as we started moving.

   A million thoughts were flying through my mind, but the only thing I could do was shout for my mom, "I'm here, baby, I am right next to you." I was scared

97

and angry about how we were getting treated. It was war, however. We were lucky even to make it this far. I wondered what Dad was doing and how he was feeling. I tried to focus on surviving and being with my mom. While we were riding, I could feel the enormous potholes and ditches that were swaying us back and forth. I could hear the disgusting, vulgar jokes the drivers telling. I was terrified. *Were we going to make it? Was I ever going to see Dad again?* Tears fell down my cheeks, and I closed my eyes. The bouncing around in the van was horrible. We were going over the tops of rocks and ditches. I heard bullets and grenades in the distance, but none falling close to us. The soldiers had a route through territory they occupied, so they knew no one would be shooting at them.

How was Dad going to go back to our neighborhood? God, I was terrified. I hoped they'd help him get out and see us. We were riding for what seemed about a half an hour before the van stopped. The door opened, "Look at them. They are blind pigs." The soldiers grabbed us and threw us onto the ground, untying our hands and taking off the bags. I scratched my knees and face. We were in the Serbian base, up in the mountains. The soldier above me wore a huge eagle sign on his hat, and a Serbian flag called a 'kokarda.' He was the lieutenant, amused to see us powerless and on the ground.

He smirked, "What are your names?" My mother replied, "Mirjana." As she dropped her head down, I listened as she lied about her name. If they found out that she was Muslim, they would cut her throat right then and there. She used the name of my father's sister. I guess that was the first name that came to her. Ana gave her name too, and the rest of ours. The lieutenant smiled, "Get up, my Serbian women and children. We need to transport you to the base, and then we'll get you out in the morning." The base had tents set up. It was a whole functioning village with people smoking meat and soldiers drinking. It seemed like there was no war going on at all, at least in this side of town. They had everything, all in green, camouflaged military-style tents.

There were a lot of civilians there too, all the Serbians that had nowhere to go. There were women there, serving the soldiers. It was unbelievable. They had tanks, bazookas, military trucks, artillery, and all kinds of guns. They were equipped well, compared to TO. It was night and day. As they gained power, the Serbs had taken all of the Yugoslavian army equipment to take over the city and state. Some of the war machines were impressive. It was terrifying. These were the weapons that were destroying our city; Those vicious machines were in the hands of these cruel people. Yet, here we were, escaping through their territory. It was a lot to grasp for a young mind, but I was becoming more mature every day.

The soldiers took us to a tent. As we were walking, they looked at us, and again I got that nasty feeling in my stomach. I was scared to stay here, even for a minute. They might torture us or do anything they wanted with us. Also, if they found out that Mom was Muslim, we would all die. As we walked further, I noticed that – amid the many green tents – there was one that was yellowish-brown. I wondered why it was different. Then we were stopped in front of it, and my heart dropped. Soldiers came out of that tent bullying women, pushing them and dragging them. The women had half of their clothes ripped off. Some of them had their breasts half out and covered in cuts, bruises, and blood. They looked like they have been raped and beaten continuously.

Mom froze, her hand in mine was instantly wet with cold sweat. She grabbed me tighter to her chest. I stopped breathing for a second: *Did we go into a trap? Was this "escape" actually the path to imprisonment?* Our leading soldiers said to the post soldier, "These are our Serbian women and children. I'll come back to have some of those Balije." *Balije* was a term they used for Muslims. The soldiers waved us to go on as it all clicked in my head: *they had Muslim women and children there as sex slaves and workers*. I couldn't even look at those women.

99

They had their heads down, and their eyes were full of tears and blood. Their souls were gone entirely. I couldn't imagine the horror they were going through. People like my mom tortured like this because of their Muslim names. My heart hurt so badly for them. I was devastated but couldn't ignore the fact that I was glad it was not us.

We couldn't give up. We needed to survive, but I felt a deep hatred toward these 'Serbian pigs,' even though my father had a Serbian name. I wondered if we knew any of those women if any of them survived the physical and mental abuse. The thoughts going through my mind were flurrying so fast that I was nauseous and dizzy. However, we kept walking, hoping to make it to a safe tent and leave this place tomorrow. They took us to what they called "the refugee camp" and gave us food and let us wash up. There were at least fifty other refugees there, all Serbian women and children, all looking as frightened as we were. None of them talked to us. Everyone kept to themselves. Most women were with younger children, but there were some older girls there, too. Most of them looked like they were from the villages, but some were from the city. It was strange. None of them said a word, as if they knew they could not trust anyone. No one even made eye contact. We did the same.

There were some beds, and we were told to stay there until we left the mountain in the morning. We ate some bread and meat and just waited. The night came quickly. However, the sound of grenades and bullets sounded different that night. The weapons were less intense because they were launched from here into the city. It was a lot for me to swallow that these animals were the ones killing us down there, shooting at my dad, and yet here we were. Rage bubbled in my stomach, but then the fear and a survival instinct made me cry quietly. I hugged Mom, who was on the alert every second. She kept praying that morning would come soon so we could leave. As the night progressed, Mom and Ana spoke quietly, and so did the other women. Igor didn't look scared. Seeing that in him gave me a little bit of courage. He told me to hold on and that everything would be fine. He also asked me if I had seen the massive guns. I guess for a thirteen-year-old boy, that was fun and intriguing.

Things seemed to be okay until we heard loud country music and the laughter of drunken soldiers. That's when a sad silence came over our tent. You could not hear anyone breathing. We could hear the agony and screams of the Muslim and Croat women in the other tent, along with the laughter of the men abusing them. Their screams and cries made tears roll down our faces. It was dehumanizing. I clasped my hands over my ears and imagined Dad and our old house. Mom covered my head, too, trying to stifle the screams. My nerves could barely take the stress of that night. I dreamt of my dad. I wished he was there with us. I missed him so much. My soul hurt. I needed to know he was okay.

We were woken by a siren and soldiers entering the tent, "Get up. Get up! Time to go." I was scared by the siren, but Mom tried to soothe me, "It's okay, baby." Ana helped us get on the move,   "It's just time to go. We need to get out of this base." Her confidence made me a little calmer, and we got up. The soldiers told us to make a line as they walked us to the trucks. I shivered in the chilly mountain air. The woods were damp, and we lined up like animals. They had nasty smirks on their faces. I guess the guns made them feel powerful. I hated them, and I hated seeing them. They let ten men out of the truck. All dressed in civilian clothes with their hands tied behind their backs. The soldiers shoved them behind the last tent in the village. I supposed they were Muslim and Croat men. My heart dropped: *Where were they taking them?* These were the people they found in the neighborhoods while they were ethnically cleansing. We heard the soldiers telling them, "You fucking balije! Line up!"

They took the men deeper into the woods, where we could not see them

---

anymore. As the soldiers pushed us toward the truck, I heard automatic machine gun fire – distant but powerful. I knew those bullets were taking the lives of all of those men. That was it. They had killed them all. I couldn't believe it, right then and there and with no remorse, they killed all of those prisoners. We all started weeping. I was in shock; horror engraved its essence deep within me. We were in a nasty, horrible war, and there was no ignoring it. My flight or fight instincts kicked in again. All we could do was strive for escape. Mom whispered, "Honey, we will get out. Just keep walking." I was still numb, but I knew I had to go on. We had to get out. I held Mom's hand and imagined that I was going to see my dad, which gave me the strength to go on.

The trucks were military-style transporters, like big pickup trucks with green canvas roofs. They stacked all of us in. Each vehicle only fit a few people, but they forced us in like animals. There was nothing we could do but go along. These men were not there to comfort us; they were there to torture us. They followed their orders, but I believe – if it were up to them – they would have raped and tortured us all. We just kept quiet and endured the rough handling. Mom didn't let them touch me to get me in the truck, but I remember they squeezed her arm so hard that she screamed as it left a bruise. They stacked us and squeezed us all into two trucks. The children were stumbled over and crying. There just wasn't enough room for all of us. We piled on the dirty floor, and I sat on Mom's lap. We were scared and wet, mud all over everyone, but we were alive and getting out of this hell.

Mom held me as hard as she could. Ana held Igor too. We feared we were going be massacred in the dark trucks. It was hard to breathe. All we could smell was the woods and the diesel from the vehicles, which turned on with a frightening rumble. The trucks were powerful and took off without hesitation. The minute they began rolling, we started inhaling dirt. The roads were rough, dug up secret pathways. We could not see anything because they closed the canvas. We bounced all over the place, piled up that every jump hurt as our weight transferred from one body to the next. We were all screaming aloud; mothers cried and held their children. Mom protected me as much as she could, taking the brunt of the hits.

I don't remember the women and children's faces, but I'll never forget their cries and moans. My adrenaline was rushing. All I could think was to hold on, hold on, and we would make it. The rocking truck kept stirring up dirt, making us all cough. It was getting harder to breathe. Mom was choking on the smoke. I just kept squeezing her arms. I couldn't even see Ana or Igor. I started to pray that we would survive this ride. We were all hoping it would be over soon but had no idea how long it would take. I didn't know exactly where we were going, but I knew it was further and further away from Dad. The soldiers weren't trying to drive carefully, and the roughness was as bad as could be. We were speeding over holes and dirt piles and going like that for what seemed like hours.

Then, all of a sudden, we hear a loud boom. The truck swerved, almost flipping on one side, then the other. It was horrifying. We all screamed at the top of our lungs, holding on for dear life. We were up on two wheels for a moment, and I thought to myself that we were going to die in a crash, not by a grenade. The driver struggled to get the truck under control, so we ended up on four wheels again and finally stopped. The smell was awful, the burning tires, dirt everywhere. We were choking. We heard soldiers yelling outside, and we were all screaming. As they opened the canvas, we squinted into the light. They yelled for us to get out of the truck and opened the gate. Mom was coughing so hard that she was choking. Ana was trying to help us get out. As scared as we all were, I think we were all relieved that we didn't crash and that we finally stopped.

Getting out, however, we were like a whole herd of buffalo trying to fit through a small exit. Women were crawling over each other, stepping on kids and pushing, holding each other down so they could get out first. It was a madhouse. The only reason we didn't get killed in the process was Mom and Ana holding us back, knowing that we needed to let the hysterical people out first. It was horrible. Children were screaming because they were getting hurt, they were falling out of the truck head first, and their cries were unforgettable. I was so terrified. All of us got hurt, shoved so hard that we all screamed. Igor was screaming too.

The soldiers tried to quiet the women down by pointing their guns and telling everyone to calm down. They even threatened to shoot some women that were not settling down fast enough. I don't blame them. The women were going crazy. God knows what they went through already. The soldiers screamed for all of us to get out. They told us that the truck's tire had blown up and that we needed to unload the weight. We slowly started to calm down until we heard shots fired in the distance. One of the soldiers shot in the air to warn us, "Shut up, you stupid pigs. You are too loud. You'll get us all killed. " I felt nauseous, and I couldn't breathe right. I had heard shots before but, this time, they sent crippling chills down my spine. We finally got out of the truck and stumbled over the rocks and dirt. I didn't let go of Mom's hand. She held me as tight as she could, covering me and pulling me close. I could smell smoke on her. She looked terrified, eyes red from the smoke. I felt disgusted, and hatred for everyone that made us go through this.

She saw how terrified I was, "I am here for you. Don't you worry. We will get through this." Mom always knew what to say. Her smile made me feel better, but the smoke and the foggy mountain brought back that cold, lost feeling. We got up and listened to the soldiers direct us, "We need to continue on foot from here; no other trucks are coming, we need to move along." We looked at each other: *how in the world were we going to get through these mountains on foot?* We had no other choice, however. The soldiers did not waste a minute. They started marching, leaving behind anyone that did not move along quickly.

There was no sign of life deep inside these woods. The trees were thick, fog misting through the air like ghosts. As terrifying as it was, these were the same woods we used to play in with our family. The forest was intimidating, but we needed to go through them to get out, and it was the scariest thing. I was full of adrenaline again. The idea was harder to digest – dying out there in the woods of hunger, thirst, or animal attack – instead of being shot by a grenade or bullet. None of this was what an average 10-year-old thinks about frequently, but my priorities had changed. It was all about survival.

Chapter Fourteen

Since we were some of the last ones to get out of the truck, there was a considerable distance between us and everyone else. None of us were worried, however, about not being able to follow the soldiers. We were just tired and knew that, somehow, we would get through. We followed those in front of us like robots. No words, just walking. Ana held Igor, and I held Mom. The woods were nerve-wracking. Every little noise startled me, as though a bear was coming. My heart was in my throat, but I had to concentrate so as not to fall going through the thick woods.

Everything was gloomy in the woods as if the forest was crying too. The trees all seemed intact, except for the deep ditch and road that the Serbian soldiers had excavated for their escape road. There were piles of dirt on either side of the trench. We all knew that, if we followed the path, it was sure to lead somewhere. There were fallen branches and moss everywhere. The birds were not singing like they used to, back when we played in the woods. I guess the animals had fled too.

All of us went along as fast as we could. It got chillier as we got higher into the mountains. We heard the distant soldiers yell, and an occasional scream as women and children stumbled as they struggled. I kept thinking of my family and me, coming to these woods for fun – and look at me now, using these woods to save our lives. I had never thought these woods would save my life one day. I tried to think of anything positive, just like Dad told me, "You can always find something good in any situation to focus on." I missed him so much that it hurt to think of him. It created a knot in my chest, but I just squeezed Mom's hand as hard as I could.

I tried to keep my mind occupied by thinking of the fun stuff we used to do: volleyball, mushroom picking, and just being in these woods. It helped, but I was still scared to death. Mom kept asking me if I was okay. She and Ana were talking about following the road, and Igor and I listened. He was next to me, both of us in the middle of our moms as we walked between the tall pine and evergreen trees. Climbing over fallen branches and trees left a lot of sap on our hands. The smell of fresh woods and pine was so different than it had been back when I was here to play in these woods.

We walked for what seemed an hour or two, and we were getting tired. My feet felt heavy, but the road just kept going, as if we were not getting closer to anything. It was discouraging, but we continued with what little hope we had. The sun snuck its way through the branches and hit our faces. The people right in front of us were still there, but the large crowd in front seemed to disappear. Then we heard a rumbling sound from behind. It was a small white truck with a picture of sausage and meat on it, driving up the mountain at us. At first, we were scared, not knowing what to expect, so we hid away off the road: *were we going to get killed in these woods?* There were no soldiers to tell them that we were with them. I hid behind Mom. The trucker saw us, stopped, and got out.

He was an older man, with gray hair and a beard, "Do you guys need a lift? I'm heading to the next base." We were very reluctant and must have looked so scared, "Don't worry. I will help you. I have a wife and children that I sent out of here too. I won't hurt you. I am just transporting the meat." I will never forget this man. He smiled and waved for us to come on over. I looked at Mom as Ana went forward first, "We need a ride. We were in a truck that broke down from the 7th division." The man nodded, "No problem. I am heading to their next base. I work in Base Ljubovica." Ana looked at us and told my mom, "It's okay. We will be okay." He said that he would have to put us in the back, "That's the only way you will fit."

We walked to the truck, and I realized that it was a meat refrigeration truck. We were going to be in the back with the meat, enclosed. I was terrified. The man said, "I don't have a load now, only a little box, so I will not need too much refrigeration. I will keep opening the doors so you can have some air until we get there." It was surreal; we climbed into the meat truck, with no idea if we were ever going to get out. I squeezed Mom's hand and tried to say something, but nothing was coming out. Mom looked scared, but reluctantly said, "It will be okay, honey." Ana also bent down and told me, "We will be okay. We need to try." Even though the older man looked harmless, like he was genuinely trying to help, we were suspicious and scared. Mom held me so hard that my shoulders almost fell off. Inside a meat freezer, it was cold and smelled horrible. There was a box in the back, and we stayed away from it. The truck was dirty and smelled nauseating. The man smiled as he closed the doors. Even though there was a small glass window, it got dark in there – and colder and colder by the minute.

We hugged each other and hoped that we would get out of this alive. Ana and Igor came over, and we all hugged and started crying out of both relief and fear. We all sat down next to each other and prayed. The man started the truck, and we were on our way, going over bumpy dirt up to the mountain. We could feel every curve, but not as bad as we could in the military truck. We still had to hold on tight. It was hard to breathe in there. We didn't have much air, and the smell was horrible. Also, it was so cold that it was physically hard to take in a breath. I kept gasping for air. We heard voices outside; perhaps the military soldiers saluting the man, but the truck did not stop. Our prayers were heard. We didn't want to encounter any soldiers. We were out of place and could have gotten killed so easily.

The truck kept going for what seemed like an eternity. We all thought that maybe the man was taking us to a slaughterhouse where we would all die. The panic attacks kept coming over us, with every curve and every passing moment. Ana didn't look at ease, which was the worst thing. She was our rock, the one that knew the most and had the most connections. She had taken a chance climbing in as well. We were living those moments on edge. *Where will he take us, and what will happen?* As cold as it was, we were all sweating out of pure fear. Looking back, I wonder how we even could have sweat or cry because we drank so little water. We just kept going and praying. We knew we had to try, instead of being stuck in the woods. We were not sure if we passed the other women and children, or where the soldiers took them. All we knew was that we were going wherever this man was taking us.

Still, to this day, I wonder if we ever passed those other women and children and, if we did, why didn't we stop for them. I still wonder what happened to them. All I could think about at that moment, however, was trying to breathe and get out of there alive. Suddenly, the truck stopped, and we heard the man open the back door, "I am opening the doors for you to get some air." We all leaned toward the outside and inhaled the fresh and warmer air. We stood there for a minute or two until he said that we needed to keep going. That was enough for us. We went back into the darkness of the truck, and he opened the door for us four more times.

He gave us some fresh-tasting water to drink too. We were thirsty and hungry. I could feel my ribs poking me, a constant reminder of how much I wanted good, fattening food. *What had happened to the chubby girl?* I was almost a skeleton now. Physically, I was hanging in there, but your mind starts wandering when you are in a dark, unknown place. You pray for your life. Your spirit either gives up or it gets stronger. You have to deal with reality as it gets surreal but, as long as you have some glimpse of hope, you keep going, you keep hoping. Mom had me, and I had her and Dad, who promised me that he would get out and see us again. I needed to keep the same promise and get out of here alive to see him.

I dozed off in the truck for a few minutes, but I was startled awake the next time the man opened the door for us. As we kept traveling, I heard Mom and Ana whispering to each other, though I couldn't discern what they were saying. I was too exhausted to think. I know they were talking about a plan and what they needed to do next. Igor was next to me, just staring. It didn't bother me at all, and it was reassuring. He kept talking about how some day he would rescue his dad and punish all of these evil people. That this wasn't fair, he asked me again if I saw the machine guns the soldiers had, and I answered yes. After a while, we got used to the smell of the truck, if not the cold. We heard occasional grenade detonations, more like rocket launchers.

We were at the mercy of this man. I am not sure how long the ride took, but finally, we stopped. I knew right away that this stop was different. There was a barricade that we had to go through, and they let us through. We heard the soldiers and then a lot of voices and music. I guessed we were at a base, and we all hoped we were at the right one. My heart was in my throat again. We had no idea what to expect, but the man opened the door and said, "This is Base Ljubovica. Just come out and go to the tents in the end, and you will find what you are looking for." We got out of the truck behind a tent, so nobody even saw us get out. It was strange, but we were there. We looked at Ana, and she said that this was the right place, "This is where we can take a bus out to Serbia." The driver said the same thing and, "May God keep you safe. It was my pleasure to help you." We all thanked him profusely. He seemed so out of place, almost like he wasn't real. An angel sent to help us. Still, to this day, I believe he was sent to help us out of nowhere. I thank that man wherever he is. Igor and I waved to him and whispered our "thank you." He got into his truck and left. It was a short and amazing encounter, and yet another inexplicable miracle that guided us to safety.

We were relieved to be at the base, but still extremely worried about making it out of there. At least this wasn't a slaughterhouse or concentration camp. This base was more relaxed-looking then the other one, and there were not as many soldiers walking around, but I still had that knot in my stomach. I didn't feel that we were safe or that we were about to escape. We saw some tents and some actual buildings too. This new town had bus routes that lead in and out. It looked like it had a regular order of life except that it was a base that supplied the terror of the war. That was confirmed when we saw the heavy artillery all around the town: huge tanks, grenade launchers, rifles, and bazookas. We stood there. We had no idea where to go or who to trust. Ana walked us toward the tents to find a bus, "From now on, we are on our own, and we need to be very close to each other and be careful. We need to get out of here as fast as we can." Her words were not reassuring. From that moment on anything could have happened

We gathered our strength and started marching to the tents. They looked like security checkpoints to get into the bus station. Around the tents, some buildings looked intact. I guess nobody was grenade launching and shooting at them up here, while they were destroying everything underneath them. There was a big tent that had a banner on it that read, "*Refugee Camp*." I tugged on Mom's hand when I saw that: *Was this the refugee camp that we were going to? Was this where the trucks were going? Were all of those poor women and children here?* Mom looked at me, "Don't worry. We will not end up there. We are getting out of here. I promise." I knew, however, that she could not know for sure. Everything was out of her control, but her words made both her and I feel better. I kept looking behind me as we were walking. I saw women and children going inside, but what disturbed me was the sight of an older woman being escorted there by a soldier.

Just as I was turning around, Mom pulled me. We hear a truck and commotion behind us. There were a few soldiers that came out of the truck and started yelling to the other soldiers, "The other shipment didn't come yet! We need to go for more tomorrow!" The place was soundless for a torture house, but I didn't want to imagine what happened there. Hearing men referring to women and children as a 'shipment' was not a reassuring thing. Then I saw a look on Mom's face that sent shivers down my spine. She thought the same thing. *Were we supposed to end up there? Were we 'the shipment?' The fresh meat?* She squeezed my hand and pulled me tighter, "Let's go. We need to get out of here as soon as we can." Ana pulled us closer, "The children are not to say a single word." She and Mom needed to say that they were married to Major Petrovic and Major Lazarevic, "We are here to deliver goods back to Serbia." My heart stopped; we were risking our lives on a lie. I wanted to die, I felt so horrible, but the adrenaline kept me going. We had to be strong. We had to survive and make the lie work. We had to trust Ana and ourselves.

We continued toward the security point, not taking any chances. Whatever that camp was, we didn't want to find out. We just wanted to get out, even if the camp was just a place of refuge. I just kept thinking about escape with my heart in my throat. To this day, I do not know if that was a torture camp or just a camp where refugees found a place to live. I still don't know if those other women and children made it to the base if they died in the woods. I couldn't even think about it. I was too nervous and scared. With that fear and paranoia, we continued walking, watching every corner – worried that every person was going to take us away.

Escaping the streets of Sarajevo was devastating, but this was even harder. We were in their territory, helpless. We kept walking, Mom's and my hands sweated so profusely. I couldn't understand where the sweat was coming from. Ana huddled us together, and we continued walking briskly, but not fast enough to

---

seem suspicious. A few women and children were walking around as well, but you could tell that they belonged in the village. They were not from the city. On every side, there were huge tanks, machine guns, grenades, and big rockets they called "Pigs."

We finally came to the security check. I was so nervous, I felt the ground beneath me crumble, and I just held Mom tighter. The soldiers stopped us and searched us. I absolutely hated that. I tried to block out how much they were touching me. They took us in to see an officer with a long beard and wearing camouflage. His hat bore the huge eagle sign of the Serbian republic. His accent was Serbian, and he proceeded to ask us questions. Ana jumped to it right away, answering everything. She was confident and explained everything quickly and with no issues. She was good at that. I guess, working as a diplomat, it came naturally to her. I was so nervous that I couldn't even hear them talk, but he took a long time questioning her and sizing her up and down.

Finally, he took out a pad and gave her a piece of paper, like a prescription, and sent us in the direction of another tent. Mom didn't say a word until, just as we were walking out, the captain asked Mom, "Hey, you. Blondie? What's your name?" She knew she had to use my aunt's name, and Mom smiled as she said it so naturally, "Mirjana." He regarded her a moment before saying, "Nice name." Mom walked out, pulling me so tight to her. *Was that a close call? Or just a pig trying to hit on my mom?*

Either way, I would have killed him if I could. Instead, we walked into another tent. There were a few officers there, and Ana went up to one of them. She gave them the paper, and they exchanged a few words before she came back to us. She said that the bus didn't leave for Belgrade until the next day. We would have to spend the night there

, not the best news, but we were relieved to hear that we were approved to leave. That paper made everything look legitimate. We just needed to be here for one night. They even had some food and water and mattresses. Igor was scared, and he didn't want to stay at all, "Why can't we just get a head start and leave now?" Ana just held him, "We will leave in the morning. We have no other option, honey." She took Mom and Igor's hands and led us out of the tent. Outside, she came close to us, "I am sorry, I didn't envision this going this way, but we will make it. We will get out of here. It hasn't been easy, but it could have been worse. We could have ended up in a concentration camp. I'm sorry, but we will be okay." She gave us a big hug, but she gave us something more too: *hope and reassurance*.

We walked to the waiting tent, which was in front of the bus station. We saw where they chopped all the trees down to have a better view to place their weapons. We were able to see the whole of Sarajevo like it was in the palm of our hand. All of us were mesmerized, and just naturally walked toward a small little opening, where there was half of a dead tree for us to hold on to and look down at Sarajevo. Naturally, Sarajevo was in a valley, nestled amongst all the mountains. We could never have gotten enough of that view. For a minute, everything seemed so quiet and harmonious. All I could see was the beautiful city of Sarajevo with all of its trees, buildings, roads, mosques, and churches. It was beautiful and yet very sad. For just that moment, we didn't feel like we were in a war, but back in those old times when we were on an excursion in the mountains in peace.

Shouts coming from soldiers broke the silence as Serbian folklore music started to play. I jerked back to reality, and that's when I took another look at Sarajevo. All I could think of was Dad, down there by himself. My entire family was down there, my grandma, cousins, and everyone. My heart was hurting so badly that I wanted to die. Mom's eyes were full of tears as she gazed upon the entire side of the mountain, covered in endless rows of tanks, bazookas, snipers, and intimidating rockets – all pointing to the city. That was the heavy artillery that has been pounding Sarajevo. They were destroying our city and our family. I was so mad and scared for Dad. All I wanted was to take him with us.

Ana told us that she knew it was hard to be here and see all of this, but we could not act suspicious. We had to be forceful. We all got up and got ourselves together. I looked at the artillery again, and my heart closed up. When I turned around and looked at the view of Sarajevo now, I saw things differently. The city was ugly, destroyed, smoke everywhere, ruins, not that many trees, totally the opposite of what I envisioned just moments ago. It was surreal. It was crazy. Then I remember falling to the ground.

Chapter Fifteen

The next thing I remember was waking up in Mom's lap in a panic. I got up, and she squeezed me hard. She was in tears, asking me if I was okay. I was confused. She told me that I had fainted, but that I was okay. She asked me if I was in pain and I told her no, then I asked her why she was crying, "Nothing. Nothing. I'm just glad that you are okay." Then she lifted my shirt and looked at my back. She said that one of my wounds had some shrapnel in it. It had gotten infected, but they had treated me, cleaning it and putting antibiotic cream on it to make me better. It was not serious. I ran my hand over the wound on my side and gazed at it. How strange that I didn't feel anything at all. I guess my body was dealing with so much adrenaline that I never felt the pain.

Mom couldn't stop crying. She was devastated but kept saying, "You're okay. Don't worry." Ana and Igor came over and hugged me. Ana was very calm and collected, "You just fainted because of lack of food and water and over-stimulation. Your wound is minor, and it will heal. It had nothing to do with your fainting." She told me to relax and that everything would be fine. It was the middle of the night already. In a few hours, we would finally leave. I told Mom that I was okay, but I was worried about her. She said she was fine, and we all hugged. I sat up and curiously ran my hand over the graze, then I looked to the women and children around us. Some were sleeping, and others were up, waiting like me. They looked like refugees, but none of them seemed familiar. I had no way of knowing if those were the women and children from the other camp.

It was hard to see in the weak lantern light. Then I heard Ana quietly ask Mom, "Did he hurt you?" Mom replied, "No. Just interrogated me." I immediately jumped up, "Who???" Mom turned to me and said, "Honey, don't worry. The captain that we met before just came to ask me more questions, and everything came out fine. He helped me get you some alcohol and cream for your wound." I asked her if he was the real reason that she had been crying, but she told me it was just because I had fainted. I must have asked her fifty million times if she was okay, and she calmed down and said, "Yes, look at me in my eyes. I swear on Dad. Everything is fine. I was just scared for you and didn't like him interrogating me." I was so worried, but Mom held me tight and calmed down, which made me feel better. Ana also reassured me of everything.

I waved Igor over, wanting him closer too. He said, "It's okay. Don't worry." I also asked him what had happened, and he told me that I fainted and that the captain called my mom. She returned quickly, and he had given her alcohol and gauze. He told me that my mom was just scared for me, "She thought you got shot." I told him thank you and to please stay close to me. Still, to this day, she never told me more, but I think that the captain tried something with her. He came on to her. I don't think anything happened. At least, I've always hoped so.

Mom caressed my face, and I held her tight. Ana went and talked to some of the women there, and they seemed to make friends. I just sat there and embraced Mom, who was so relieved that I was awake and okay. She kept kissing me and telling me, "Soon, we will be out. I love you." I didn't know what time it was or when we were going to leave. I was tired, and it seemed like it was nighttime. I looked outside, through an opening in the tent and, sure enough, it was dark.

All of a sudden, a siren sounded. A war siren and we all jumped up in fear. Soon after, massive shootings began. We sat there and listened again to the destruction being unleashed on my town. All of those grenades, bazookas, and guns were shooting at Sarajevo. Boom, boom, boom. Everything was shaking. The sound was a lot stronger than ever. It was raging, horrifying, and different this time – because I wasn't scared for us. I was terrified for Dad. He was down there. My friends and my whole family were down there. They were destroying my town.

I wanted to tell Mom how I felt, how much it was hurting me to watch this. Just looking at her let me know that she already knew. She felt the same way. I tried to say something, but nothing came out but a long-winded breath. We held each other. I wanted to be down there with him, to save him, but I couldn't. There was nothing I could do. Ana and Igor came over, and we just sat down and let it all sink in: *those shots were not coming at us, we are on top of the mountain.* We just needed to stay calm and live through this night, and we would be out soon. Ana kept saying, "Let's get through this night. We will be okay. We will be okay." All I could see was Dad's face.

I woke to bright light streaming into the tent. It was morning — time for us to leave. Mom held me up, "Come on, honey. It's time." Ana and Igor were awake and ready to go. I got up as soon as I could and stood next to them. Mom handed me a piece of bread and a small cup of water. Omg, did that taste right. I was starving. I inhaled the food and water and got in line with everybody else.

The soldiers came into the tent and shouted for us to line up and move to the bus station. It was those same nasty pig soldiers. They were walking around like they were gods, looking at us like we were pieces of meat. I couldn't even look at them. The captain came out, and my hand clenched around my mom's. I wanted to kill him, but I just followed the directions from the soldiers. We all went in a line to the bus station, which was very close. The weather outside was beautiful, and the forest was gorgeous. It was strange that there were no bullet shells or grenades. It looked like nothing had happened last night. I couldn't see how Sarajevo, down the mountain, looked, but I was dying to. I wanted to know if they destroyed the whole city. My heart pumped harder. Mom asked if I was okay, and I told her that I was worried about Dad. She told me, "He is astute. He will survive, just like we survived all those attacks from before." I held on to those words. Dad was my hero, and he could survive anything. We would see him again.

We kept walking until we saw the bus in front of us. I had mixed emotions. I didn't know if I should trust this bus to take us out: *Was it going to be like the last ride?* Only our natural optimism kept us going, kept us hoping. The soldiers were right in front of the bus. As we approached, they took our names and the sheets of paper to take roll. They also made sure we didn't take anything dangerous with us – as if we had the time, opportunity, or the slightest will to sneak anything on – we all knew they just wanted to feel us again. The soldiers patted us down, and we all got aboard one by one.

We took our seats. As the bus started, three soldiers boarded and took the seats in front. They were going with us. As the bus left the base, I had my eyes stuck on the tents, military cars, and the artillery that we were leaving behind. The weapons that would continue to pound my city and family. I wondered how my aunts and uncles were doing, my cousin and Grandma Emina. I was worried sick for them, and that made me think of Grandpa Ratko. My sorrow was strong.

These roads were pretty smooth because the Serbians took over the transportation roads leading out from the mountains. Steep canyons, rocks, and beautiful trees covered our route. The way was very close to the cliff drop-offs, which was amazing and scary. As we got further away from the base, the view over the drop off showed Sarajevo more and more. The beautiful city in the valley, now full of smoke and ruins. It was gloomy and looked sad. My mind fought even the most horrifying thoughts and focused on our last vacation trip to Turkey. When we were leaving the airport, the day was sunny and pleasant. I was so happy to travel, so excited. As the plane lifted from the ground, I had smiled and watched Sarajevo disappear as it smiled back at me. My mother's voice jerked me back to reality, "Honey, are you okay? What's wrong, honey?" She sounded panicked, but I reassured her, " I'm okay, Mom. I was daydreaming."

I scratched at one of my cuts from the shattered glass. It was itchy because it was healing. I held Mom and stayed like that in her embrace. Leaving Sarajevo this time was not for pleasure. The ruins I saw from the window seemed to cry, and I cried with them. I was coming to terms with the fact that I might never come back to my city: *Would I ever see my dad again? Where is this life taking us? Where and how will we survive?* My heart broke into pieces. All I could think of was my father and my family. I didn't know what to feel or how to express it. I was mad and depressed.

The bus kept going for a long time. The trip was unusually quiet. Every once in a while, we reached a checkpoint and soldiers boarded the bus to check our papers. These soldiers were silent too, no harassing looks or behavior. We didn't know what to expect. I found out later that those soldiers were Serbian, going back to their wives and children. I guess some of the soldiers had a heart. Other than the occasional checkpoints, it was smooth. We didn't hear too many grenades, some sporadic ones in the distance along with a few shots. It was weird not to hear that. The closer we got to Serbia, the further away the war became. Just a few hours away, nobody was experiencing the absolute hell, the battle among brothers. My thoughts were confused, and I felt weak and tired. We all were. The bus hugged the road, he curvy road and it was terrifying so close to the edges. Too close for comfort. Still, I looked out of the window as I dozed off, every once in a while, making sure Mom was right next to me, holding my hand and my head.

Eventually, Mom woke me up, "Baby, we're here." Sure enough, we had stopped. It was so dark outside. I didn't know where we were or how long it had been. The street was lit up, and the bus station buildings caught my eye. Not just because there was electricity, but also because the buildings and station itself were beautiful. Those were the only lights; the rest of the area was very dark. The soldiers instructed us, "Only those getting off in Belgrade get out now. The rest stay here to continue." Mom told me, "Come on, honey. We need to get out." I got up and followed her. Mom went to Ana and Igor, hugged and kissed them so hard, and said we would be in touch. She squeezed Ana's hand, "I am in debt to you forever. Thank you." I was confused: *Why are we getting off here, alone? Without Ana? Where were we anyway? Are we safe?* I asked Mom all of this, but she shushed me, "This is where we stop, honey. Say goodbye. We will see them soon."

I felt rushed, full of questions, and confused – but I followed Mom. My heart was racing, but I trusted that Mom had a plan of her own from here. She gave me a reassuring look, and I hugged them both so hard and told them I loved them. They both seemed to know the plan. I guess I was too young to understand, or Mom didn't want to overwhelm me anymore. Either way, we got out so fast. I was still in shock. Other women came out as well, and there we were. The bus didn't waste any time, and we waved goodbye to them as they left. At that moment, I felt so alone like we had parachuted into another reality. I missed them, and I missed my Dad. It was scary.

I felt like I was a robot, with legs only programmed to carry me because Mom pulled me along: *Why did we leave them so abruptly? Where were Ana and Igor going, and what will happen to them? Why didn't she tell me the plan?* I kept pulling her hand. She stopped for a minute and kneeled on the floor. With crying eyes, she told me, "Honey, I'm sorry, but we had to split up. We can't go where Ana is going. Nobody there will help a Muslim. We have to stay in this part of Belgrade. Our best man and woman live here, and they will hide us and help us. Do you remember Vania and Nenad? They have a daughter, Radica, that is your age. It will be fun. We will be okay." I listened, but she seemed more nervous and scared more now than when we were in the heart of the war.

Then it hit me; I was not just sad anymore. I was terrified too. Mom and I were in the heart of the enemy land now. A Muslim woman without her husband, with no family, no help, no friends that we were sure we could trust. We were refugees with nothing. Mom's hands were shaking. She was sweating, and I was numb. Nearby, was a blonde woman waving to us and signaling us to come over. I remembered her face. It was Vania, my mom's maid of honor. We grabbed our little bag and headed toward her. Vania was happy to see us, and she hugged Mom. Then she hugged me and said how big I looked. Mom held her tight and shed a tear. I know she was scared.

Soon we got into her car, and Vania started driving us to her house. I was in the back seat, dozing off as I listened – but didn't understand – their conversation. When Mom woke me up, it was to go into the house. We went through another room to get to ours, and then I just passed out. Little did I know that that stay in this forsaken house would be one of the worst memories and tortures of my life. I would encounter a different horror here than the grenades and bullets of war. I was about to endure the mental abuse of the brainwashed Serbian population toward refugees.

Chapter Sixteen

We woke up to a quiet, sunny morning. Mom was next to me, which was the only thing that felt secure. She kissed me, "Let's get up and say hello to everyone." We got dressed, used the bathroom, and proceeded out of the room. It was awkward because that bedroom was next to another one. So, we had to go through another bedroom to get out. Nobody was there, at the moment, thank goodness, and we exited the house. The courtyard contained two structures, one right smack next to the other. As we walked toward the other house, Vania came out to greet us. She was friendly and full of smiles. Right behind her was her husband and their daughter, Radica.

Radica was a skinny, pretty blue-eyed, little girl who you could tell by the judging look she gave us was very stuck up. They greeted us, and we ate well for the first time in so long. The meat casseroles, potatoes, and a fantastic dessert, prepared by Radica's grandparents, tasted like heaven. We shared our living quarters with Radica's grandparents. They were all interested in the conflict in Bosnia. We enjoyed the food and, for the first time in so long, some peace.

While the adults talked and seemed to be enjoying themselves, Radica came to me and asked me lots of questions that I answered truthfully. Some were normal girl things about what I liked and what my favorite games were, but some questions were about the war and the battles in Bosnia. To these war questions, my truthful answers did not match up with what they believed, or what Serbian propaganda was telling – or instead brainwashing – the people with, even little girls like Radica. That's how our differences started. That's when it hit me what it was going to be like to live like a refugee.

To make a long story short, Radica hated me, mostly because of the pure fact that she idolized and loved Serbian soldiers and leaders like Radjacic, who would later be convicted of massive genocide by the international governance committee in 2012. He ended up committing suicide due to the guilt he felt from murdering millions of innocent people. Radica, however, thought that he was a hero, conquering the land that was taken away by extremist Muslims and Croats. She felt that he was defending the Serbian Bosnians from the wrath of Muslim attacks.

I couldn't understand how she could think that. I wanted to open her eyes to what truthfully happened, that it was Serbians who displaced me and killed many friends and family. They were terrorists too. I wanted to show her that all sides not only Serbians were guilty and the war was dirty, with destructive people on either side. I wanted to show her that only love and understanding can help this situation and not extremism. I was so angry that I fought with her, trying to make her understand. Unfortunately, her state of mind was such that she didn't want even to fathom the concept. What was worse was that her parents and grandparents thought the same, so, from the very beginning, they resented Mom and me because of our views.

Now we were being seen as scum, refugees that were poisoning their state, low lives that should go back or die. This attitude reflected on everyday things, and the resentment increased more and more every day. From that day on, every time Radica would have friends over, I was never allowed to be near them or talk to them. They would draw a line on the floor that I couldn't pass because I was a refugee that didn't like the Serbs. She would separate from me from her friends by opening an umbrella so that I could not look in. She'd hide behind that umbrella and play. I was not allowed to be near them. I was forced to be on my own while Mom looked for work during the summer. I would sit on my own, use the little pen and paper that I had, and draw pictures of my dad. I missed him so much.

I wasn't even allowed to use her crayons. One time I tried to borrow some, and Radica threw herself on the floor, and her mom took them away and washed them with soap and water. It was horrible. I felt like a leper. Once, Radica had a fashion show at school. All the kids at the play received a goodie bag. Except me, of course. It was tough to swallow. Everybody looked at me like an alien. At their house, the tension was terrible and growing. The grandparents were mean and strict with us. We couldn't get up in the middle of the night to use the bathroom because it would bother them. We could not talk or make any noise, or they would get furious. Vania would not be as mean, but even she mistreated us. I remember using the window to get in or out of our room, sometimes to go pee outside without bothering the grandparents.

We lived as unwanted roommates that barely had any contact with them. Dinners were the worst. They would not say anything while we ate. At some point, they must have had good intentions toward helping us, but those feelings couldn't compete with the brainwashing. They wanted us out of their house, mainly because they were getting derogatory comments from their neighbors. It didn't help that perhaps neighbors knew that my Mom was Muslim or had a Muslim name. It was hard to deal with that hatred and pressure every day. I would try to go with Mom to town, while she looked for help and connections. We had no money or anything else but hope. We used to go to town to try to get in contact with Dad, or for my mom to contact her company to help us with accommodations and food and money. We needed to take the bus and borrow money to eat.

One day, however, we went to an office and got to talk to Dad for the first time. We only had a batch of bananas. That was our meal for the whole day. Our hunger didn't matter, though, because we got to talk to Dad, and he was okay. He was still in Dobrinja, but he reassured us that everything was okay and he was safe. I couldn't stop crying when I heard him but, as much as we were suffering here, I couldn't tell him anything because I knew he was worse off. It was fantastic hearing from him. He was alive. My heart hurt for him; the only way I could cope was to imagine that he was just on another business trip and that he would be back soon. I couldn't think any other way; especially not that he was in a living hell in which he could so quickly die. He talked to Mom for a little longer, and I could tell by the look on Mom's face that he told her some tough things that he was going through. I wondered if he was getting threatened by the TO, or if the situation had worsened.

After that conversation, Mom started doing everything she could to try to get him out. We spent the rest of that day holding each other tight and trying to gather the hope we needed to get us through this refugee nightmare. It seemed like everywhere she went; people did not want to help her. She didn't give up, though. She tried so hard to get us help, use her connections to get Dad out and get us fed. That's how the days went. I tried to go with her as much as I could because I couldn't stay in that house anymore. Mom wanted me with her at all cost. We were the only thing each other had.

Not long into our travels into town, Mom found us both a job to help us with the papers for travel and survival. We were ironing for a company that provided linens and rags for the hotels and restaurants. We both spent hours in a little basement ironing sheets, curtains, and covers. It was brutal work, and we both ended up covered in burn marks from the steam iron, but it was better than staying in the pressure of that house. We ironed every day for hours and got paid just enough to get a little food, maybe a new shirt and pants and anything that could help with the creation of transfer papers. Mom was determined to get us out through her company, who was willing to help place us somewhere else. It was a good thing that she knew a lot of people from her company, and they were a few angels who were willing to help.

As we worked and went all over town to get papers and secure our exit from Belgrade, Mom was also working on getting documents to get Dad out. We talked to him as often as we could. The situation there was getting awful. The Serbs were approaching Dobrinja, and it looked like they were going to take over. It was terrible news for everyone there, so Dad decided to try and get out of that neighborhood without being caught. He was going to go to our old community and see if he could find someone familiar and willing to help him survive or leave. I felt such sorrow for him. I missed him so much and prayed for him every day, but adrenaline and hardships of our own kept us focused on our survival as well.

Back at the house of hell, the situation was unfavorable. Mom barely spoke to Vania and Nenad. It was clear that they wanted us out. Radica continued with her derogatory remarks. She would try on all of these fancy clothes she had and flaunt them in front of me. It was so hurtful to a gullible eleven-year-old who only had old jeans and shirts. To add insult to injury, she would always tell me I was too fat, not pretty enough, and that her clothes would never fit me. Even though I have lost my chubbiness, I was still structurally a big girl, certainly very different than her. Radica was mean, spoiled, and hateful. I tried to keep it all from Mom, knowing that conflicts might mean the end of us here, and she already had so much on her plate. We had no other choice but to stay. One day, however, Mom heard Radica call me an "ugly piggy refugee." That comment broke the camel's back. Mom blew up at her, "You insecure, horrible piece of shit." Radica looked as though hit by a bus.

Once Mom took her frustrations out on Radica, our welcome there came to an end. Her parents came to console her and take her away from us. Vania and Nenad were furious. There was nothing left to do but leave. The adults talked about it calmly later and, from what I understood, we were not kicked out – but encouraged to leave as soon as we could. We went to bed that night, stressed and frustrated. Every night since we got out of Sarajevo, we had laid together, waiting for our lullabies to put us to sleep – the grenades we would listen to every night in the war. Our hearts were full of sorrow and hurt, which was exhausting enough to make us fall asleep holding hands.

Chapter Seventeen

For two weeks, we worked hard ironing and at different offices, getting approvals and support to leave. We used every dime on papers and permissions and spent the least amount of time in the house as we could. We ate anything we could get on the street for cheap: toast, spoiled meat, or maybe a banana if we were lucky. I remember clearly one day, as we were getting off the bus to get to our work. That day we did not know how we would eat; we did not have any money. We hoped that some miracle would happen to help us. Just as we got off the bus, an older lady was waiting to get on.

We passed right by her, and as she continued walking into the bus, a strange and eerie thing happened. There was a slight breeze that pushed through us, and I would swear that her purse opened up as if someone opened it with their hands and out of the bag a German 50 Mark bill flew out. It was so surreal, she did not notice, and mom and I did. The money flew by us in slow motion and away from the bus. We were standing there as if the time froze for a bit. I chased down the street to get the money to return it to the lady. I finally caught the money, but the lady was on the bus already. The bus was already pulling away from us, and nobody else was around. It looked like nobody else saw that but us. We looked at each other in awe. That's when I knew there was something extraordinary guiding us and protecting us. We were sent money to survive out of the blue. I will always remember that miracle. We took the money, thanked God, and went into the store to get something to eat. My mom's face said it all, hope and faith from above is what will help us always.

We talked to Dad as often as we could. As if things could not get worse, the next time we heard from him broke our hearts. He told me how much he loved me and to be safe and reliable for Mommy. His voice was cracking, and I knew something was wrong. He refused to tell me, so I just told him how much I wanted him with us and how much I loved him. Mom spoke to him for a few minutes more and then hung up. Outside the operator's office, she took me to a bench and sat me down, holding me. Her eyes were full of tears as she told me that the Serbian army had caught dad. The only reason he was still alive was his Serbian last name and a lie about being trapped by TO. He agreed to fight with their army to survive.

As soon as I heard that, I was devastated. I couldn't believe that Dad was now fighting with the scum that destroyed my home and killed people I loved. I was disappointed and too young to understand that he had to do it to survive. I couldn't believe that he was part of the Serbian army, having to kill people like Mom's family. I was hysterical and heartbroken. My hero was with the enemy. Mom tried to explain that we were lucky he was alive at all. It was a blessing that he got caught because now he had a chance to survive and leave. Otherwise, he probably could not have survived at all.

This way, he could pretend his way into food and a bunker, and possibly escape. It didn't mean that he had to kill, but he had to do whatever he could to survive. He needed to play the part, "We need him to do whatever he can so that he can come to us. Trust in your dad. He will do anything he needs to be with us. Don't be scared. Just believe in him."

That's all I could do, have faith. I couldn't think about how he would survive fighting for them. I knew they would put him on the front lines, and that his chances would be slim in this dirty war. I just hoped and prayed that he would have enough luck to make it through, without having to kill innocent people. That is when I started praying more for him every night, always through tears. I would try to analyze what he was going through. It was like a movie in my head, playing the worst-case scenarios as my anxiety grew more every day. I was devastated. Each day I would think that this would be the day that I lose my dad to those barbarians.

It was so hard for me to understand because I had lost everything to the Serbian army.

Those days were difficult for Mom and me, but we kept living. We worked hard and stayed together every moment. We would just come home late, climb in through the window, wipe ourselves with a rag and sleep. We would wake up early in the morning, use the bathroom while the older adults were in the other house, change, and go back out without having to see or speak to any of them. Sometimes we even stayed and slept on the floor in the basement where we ironed, so as not to go home. I felt like a zombie, doing everything I could to keep our minds off the misery. We worked hard and hoped for Mom's company to relocate us. None of that was harder than worrying about Dad. Not hearing from him was the worst, but all we could do was have faith.

Finally, the day came, three weeks after Mom yelled at Radica. While we were in the city, Mom's company called and said we were accepted to go to a mountain hotel, where they would help us stay and work. The resort was in the mountains of Zlatibor, two hours from Belgrade. We were delighted to leave the house of torture. That very morning, Radica had pushed me while Mom was in the bathroom and said her parents were going to kick us out and let us rot in the street. I was so angry but, at the same time, I felt sorry for her. I didn't react. I just turned and walked out. Physically I was okay, but emotionally, she scarred me forever. Scarred me into thinking that I was not good enough, pretty enough, and never welcome or capable of having friends or love again. Mom didn't know anything about it. So, when I heard the news of the move to Zlatibor, it was like a rebirth for me. I felt like going away would give me the strength to see Dad, and

131

the hope that he would escape the Serbs. I worried about all of our other family, who we were able to speak to only sporadically with the operator. They were all surviving as best they could. I worried about Njanja, my cousins, and everybody else. Amidst those worries, I always shed many tears remembering Grandpa Ratko.

Mom explained that we would go to the hotel and they would help us there. We would need to take a bus, then her friends and long-time colleagues would settle us in. She had also been working on getting Dad out, too, which gave me hope and strength. Mom was my everything, my hero.

As liberating as it was to leave, it still meant that we were going into another unknown. As scary and terrifying as it was, the unknown had become the norm for us. At least we were getting away from Radica. We packed and said goodbye to everyone, as our bus was leaving the next morning. I hated going back to the house, but I could bear it if it were the last time. The first thing Mom did was break the news to them, and they were so happy. You could tell. Next, just to make a point and give them something to feel guilty about, she said to them that Dad had joined the Serbian army. Their eyes lit up, and they were so glad. Mom held my hand tighter. Radica's grandpa saluted us and told us that my dad was welcome there as "our soldier," and that he was proud of him. Those were the first words he ever spoke to us. Now we were heroes in their minds because Dad was in the Serbian army. Mom later told me that it was okay to lie this time, about the circumstances of Dad serving for the Serbs. They didn't deserve honesty. I kept quiet, and we went on to pack. It was sad the amount of brainwashing there was in Serbia. That final night, however, Mom's lie helped to relieve the pressure. I couldn't even look at Radica's face, but I bet she felt terrible, that is if she had a trace of goodness in her heart.

That's how many people lived in that region during that period, in hatred inside their obtuse bubble. The whole city seemed to be like that. It's no wonder why the war broke out in my country. How easily people can forget who they are. How quickly family and friends can become enemies. That's what was the worst. As we ate dinner, they were all a little friendlier and more talkative, but Mom and I did the usual: ate, packed, and went to bed. The next morning, we said quick goodbyes. I even hugged Radica before we made our way to the bus. We were happy to get the road under us and leave that city of hatred behind.

Chapter Eighteen

The ride was not that long, but I still found the time to doze off. The pure mental exhaustion was enough to put an elephant to sleep. We were worn out. I woke up just before the bus pulled up to Zlatibor, a small village and resort in the Serbian mountains. and the beautiful nature of the mountain. The resort was in front of a big lake. I remembered Mom talking about this particular project. She had spent a lot of time traveling and helping with the construction of this one hotel. We didn't have another choice but to go there and hope that whoever promised to help Mom was trustworthy. Now I knew why she hadn't told me too much about our escape. It was too much for her to bear, a single woman with her child in a total twilight zone. I was scared again, worried about my mom. I held her hand tight, and we walked to the main entrance with one little bag.

I had so many questions, but I knew now was not the time. At that moment, Mom stopped and held me with a look that was more focused than ever, "Baby, Mommy has a few friends from work that arranged us to stay here. You will know who they are, but don't talk to anybody else. If anyone asks you who we are, or what we are doing here, you tell them that we are Serbians and my name is Mirjana. Your name is Manja." I nodded my head, even though I felt like I didn't understand anything, I knew I had to be steady and quiet as we went in. I knew I would get an explanation at some point, and now was the time to survive this stage of our lives. We stopped for a moment, took a deep breath, and took in the details of the hotel and its beauty. The entrance was perfectly manicured and lit just right. The wooden beams were constructed in an angle to give it all the feeling of a cottage, and the mountain view in the back was mesmerizing. It looked like a five-star resort in Switzerland. It had different levels, huge glass windows, and balconies, and a huge park around it. The lake illuminated it well, and the landscape's majestic trees made it look magical. As scared as I was, its beauty and charm made me feel more at ease. I had a feeling it would be better than Belgrade.

It was no surprise that the hotel had style. After all, Mom was the architect. It was nice. I couldn't believe we were going to stay here. *For how long?* Everything was very contemporary. It had open floor-to-ceiling wood-framed windows and a little fireplace in a cozy seating area with a TV. I must admit that TV must have been the best thing I had seen during this war. It brought quite a little smile to my face, even if that smile was full of anguish, confusion, anxiety, and exhaustion.

We came to the lobby, and Mom spoke to a lady in front, who called the manager. A tall, skinny man came out, older with a beard. The minute he saw Mom, he smiled wide and hugged her. He kissed me on the cheek as well and beckoned us to follow him. He took us up the elevator to our room on the second floor, away from other rooms. It looked like a cleaning crew quarters. He didn't say much, as if he couldn't. It was very awkward, and everything happened quickly. It was late at night, so we wanted to get settled in. Mom held me tight, and nothing was said as he brought us into the room. He whispered a few words to Mom and said that he would see us tomorrow. All the instructions were in the room. He hugged her, waved at me, and we went in. It was a small room with two twin beds, and it had a little window, a bathroom, and a closet. The apartment was perfect for us, with its small TV and a little desk. Mom ran to me and hugged me. We both looked at each other and cried through all the mixed emotions we had. She fell to her knees and released the first sigh of relief I had seen since the start of the war. It was a good feeling for a minute. We were far from the bullets and grenades, out of immediate danger, and out of the crazy house and Belgrade. We truly enjoyed the moment, even if we didn't know what tomorrow held for us. I didn't even know where we were really.

Mom gathered herself, went to the little desk, and sat down on the chair. She pulled out a piece of paper the man had given her and sat down on the chair to read. It was the instructions from the hotel. She read it casually, and it didn't seem to worry her – and then exhaustion caught me. I sat down. I felt so alone and lost. Mom encouraged me to take a shower and gave me a towel. I looked at that towel like it was a miracle. I felt weird, out of place. It was crazy to be in a hotel, alive, about to take a shower. As I sat there, all I could think of was Dad. My heart was breaking, and I didn't know if he was still alive. As sadness overcame me, I stood up and went into the bathroom with hopes of having a good cry under the water. Mom hugged me, kissed my forehead, and told me that, when I got back out, she would have a little snack for us.

I went in, turned the water on, and the sorrow began. The water felt incredible, and the crying felt even better as I repeatedly prayed for my dad and everyone else to survive. I hadn't had a proper shower in so long, even in the Belgrade house. There, we had to go quickly so as not to waste water. I got out of the shower and, sure enough, Mom had little chocolate wafer cookies. I guess they were waiting for us in the room. *Wow, chocolate, wafers!!* I went back to being a little kid again, so excited that we had food – and chocolate wafers at that! I couldn't process it all. I was confused and felt guilty for my dad. Scared, but yet relieved. Mom went into the shower after she made sure the door was locked, and the windows were covered. She even put a chair in front of the door. Mom told me to lay down and try to sleep, but all I could do was stare at the ceiling. When Mom came out of the shower, she looked relieved and a little better. She gave me a little kiss that instantly helped me relax a bit.

That night, all I could do was stare at that ceiling. I could not sleep at all. I remembered hearing every noise, every crack, the wind outside, even little animal noises. I felt so strange. It was anxiety, guilt, and fear, but, most of all, I realized what was missing. The lullaby I had grown so used to. I realized that I *needed* that sound of falling grenades and detonations. They had truly become my lullabies. Without them for a security blanket, I stayed awake for what seemed like the whole night, feeling desperation about whether we would ever see Dad and the rest of our family again. I was coming to terms with the fact that, while we were out of the active war zone, we were not sure how safe we were here as refugees. We saw how bad Belgrade was. Will the mountains be worse? The only thing that truly mattered to my eleven-year-old mind was that I wanted to see my dad and make it. I continued staring at the ceiling and cried as I fell asleep.

The next morning, we woke up in peace. The sunlight was beautiful, and I couldn't believe I could hear birds singing. Mom was up already. She dressed in a hotel uniform, but it was new and fresh and an upgrade from what we wore for so long. She hugged me, and the smile on her face was a welcomed surprise. I haven't seen that smile in so long that I almost forgot how it looked. I smiled too and hugged her back as she said, "Let's get dressed, baby. We need to go down and get something to eat." I was happy to hear that, and, despite being confused, I got ready and followed her without asking any questions.

Her uniform was a green t-shirt and beige pants, with the logo that said Hotel Zlatibor. I figured that we had to do what we had to do to stay here. We went downstairs into the kitchen, in the back where all the cleaning staff was. As I walked in, I absorbed all that was around me. People were giving us weird looks, sizing us up and down. Mom held me tight and held her head up high, moving to the man that led us into the hotel the night before. He greeted us and let us sit down with the crew to eat breakfast. He quickly introduced us, Mom as "Mirjana," and me as "Manja." Hearing her fake name reminded me that we needed to continue this secret life, living a lie to survive. I knew to stay quiet, as we sat down and ate pastries and juice.

We all ate quietly. There were four cleaning ladies and us. Two of them smiled and asked us where we were from. Mom responded, "From the village of Pale." Another lie to support our fictitious Serbian lives. They didn't say too much, just talking amongst themselves while Mom went to the office and spoke with the gentleman that received us. She wasn't in there long before coming back to finish breakfast. We did not say a word to each other, but we understood each other correctly. We ate in peace and, shortly after we got up, went to the supply room and got the cart with towels and cleaning supplies. As we both pushed on the cleaning cart, our hands overlapped each other's, and we pushed the cart to the lobby's bathroom.

Everything was happening so quickly. Before I knew it, I no longer take the quiet and uncertainty. I closed and locked the bathroom door and asked Mom what was going on. Her eyes were watering as she explained to me that we needed to live as cleaning ladies, doing all the physical work and whatever they told us. In turn, they would feed us and keep us safe. More than anything, they would keep our identity as Serbian. "I am so sorry, honey," she told me, "but this is the only way. You don't have to do any cleaning. Just stay with mommy here until it's time for you to start school." I looked at her with a puzzled look of sadness. It was hard for me to swallow our new reality, that Mom, the brilliant architect of this very hotel, was now having to be its cleaning lady. We had to hide and live like this until we figured out what could be our next step – and how we could include Dad. Being young helped me to accept the situation and move forward quickly. I justified it in my head, we were there and alive, and we had to do whatever it took to move on. At that moment, I felt stronger, older, and obliged to help Mom. She needed me. I needed to grow up and help. I hugged her and took the mop, "Then we will do this together," I said.

We ended up doing this every day, and we found some joy in it. We got to taste good hotel food, watch TV, and participate in the hotel's activities. We got used to cleaning toilets and scrubbing floors quick and found the best methods to do it fast. We found out son enough how nasty people were, how dirty they lived, and how humbling it was scrubbing toilets. We would get up in the morning, work all day, and then get fed. At night we would rest, read, and enjoy the amenities for a bit. My favorite activities were walks around the beautiful big lake right in front of the hotel and down into town. It had little cottage shops. We found joy in small things, and that made us stronger and more mature.

Chapter Nineteen

It has been two weeks since we had heard from Dad. At night I used to dream of him being in our room. I knew that he was still alive. I felt his presence in my heart. Mom was sad. She tried to reach Sarajevo every day, to see if Dad was there with them. The connection, however, was not going through. She also tried calling her brothers and her mom, but could not get through to them either. It was tough to imagine where he was, where all our family was. What we left behind was deeply engraved in our hearts, like carrying a heavy brick on your chest. So, the reality of the resort that we had in front of us was a mental escape. It was, but it was better than being in the war. I prayed every night for things to get better and for me to see Dad again.

To this day, I remember the ceiling of that room. I stared up at it so much that it was like my temple. Two weeks there seemed like an eternity. We were exhausted from hard work, but it was worth it because nobody was bothering us. We did hear a few derogatory comments by the other ladies under their breaths, that we were weird or didn't do the job well, but Mom kept quiet. It was not worth getting noticed or getting into a fight. We kept on, working, and hoping to see our family and Dad. The manager would check on us every once in a while. I was thankful that he did, but I didn't like him at all. I had a suspicion that he liked Mom and wanted to take her from Dad. Mom was friendly with him but stood her ground. I guess that's where I learned the art of using one's charm but up to a point. At least I wanted to believe it was that way. She explained that the manager was an old friend and coworker. He used to be her right-hand on the job, and she trusted him. I had no choice but to believe her.

There were a few times, however, that she returned from talking to him in tears. I asked if he did something to hurt her and she always said that she was sad because she couldn't reach anybody on the line. I was young, and I understood, but to this day, I don't know if anything happened to Mom. It saddens me to think about it. As a mother now, I understand a little more about the sacrifices a woman would make for her child. We were safe, had food and a roof over our heads, and a little money for clothes and any other stuff. We plugged along and continued to live. All we had was hope.

I only had a little time before they would sign me up to go to school again. Mom wanted me not to miss too much school, and the plan was to start in the village next semester. I didn't want to. I didn't want to mix with the Serbians here, and I didn't want to be alone. However, the decision was that I had to continue getting educated and have some normalcy in my life. I had about a month or so until I needed to start. I enjoyed that month as much as I could, which meant more walks to the town and window-shopping. I remember wanting this big beautiful wristwatch that I would see every time I went to the village. I could only dream of getting it, however, because it was way beyond our budget. Ironically, I hate wearing watches now, but I wanted it then. It became a symbol, of what just a short period had done to my family and me.

I used to visit the shop every day to look at the watch, hoping to one day get it – either to help me in school or to 'be my blanky.' A child's heart is so pure and innocent. Sometimes I look back and realize that being so pure had helped me get through the craziness of the war's nasty reality. The watch and walks around the lake represented spiritual escape for me, the dream that kept my little mind intact. Mom and I loved walking around the lake and sitting down on a bench to look at the reflection of the moon. The pine trees served as a protective wall, and the calm of the lake gave us breathing room. It brought us closer to serenity. I loved that lake and watching the stars that were so abundant in the mountains.

One night, as we watched the sky illuminate the lake, my heart saw hope, and I felt some relief. That night, I saw the most beautiful and long-lasting shooting star. It was so bright, and its fall so long that it was surreal. I immediately wished upon it for Dad to come back, with every cell in my body. I believed in its power. Never before had I seen a shooting star like that. We stayed and watched the lake and stars a little longer and then headed back to the hotel for bed. To get ready for another day of cleaning and serving. The next day, however, was far from peaceful. It brought another hard reality check of our situation.

That morning, Mom went to the office to try and call Dad in Sarajevo, as she did every day. I usually spent this time in the lobby or the kitchen to get a little Danish. This morning, as I waited, military men came in. They were the Serbian military savages who were destroying my city. I could not stand to look at them, and I had to be quiet. They all had beards and looked filthy. They came in loud and shaking the whole hotel. They needed to stay there. My stomach dropped. I wanted Mom close to me. They were drunk and talking nasty. What really scared me was when they started saying that they had heard there was "a Muslim piece of crap refugee" in the hotel, "We will torture and kill them right away." Those words made me die inside. I thought they had come for us, that we landed in their reach. I didn't know what to do. I stood there, frozen, and trying not to cause too much attention. I wanted to disappear.

Hearing the commotion, Mom came out with all of the hotel managers. She ran to me, while the managers tried to calm the men, assuring them that this was a Serbian hotel that does not allow Muslims. The manager offered them a drink in the restaurant, and to treat them well, "Come on over, our heroes, for a drink!" He defused the situation and took the soldiers away. Our hearts dropped. The manager signaled for us to run back to our room. Once we were there, Mom told me, "We will be okay. The soldiers will come and go. We are protected here, even on paper." I started shaking. I thought that we escaped when we left Belgrade, but the hatred was following us, even here. I was devastated.

Mom and I hugged very tight, and she told me that she spoke to Dad, "He is okay. He's settled in the Serbian base in the airport." She said that he was lucky to find people he knew in the base. They helped him while he was playing the role of a real soldier. I felt immediately better like she knew I would. A warmth came over my body, knowing that he was alive. My focus shifted away from the soldiers. I was happy to finally hear from Dad, knowing he could get through this alive and come to us one day. We stayed there for a bit, ate a little bread, and just relaxed. Mom was my strength. Eventually, we went on with our day. We made sure to go nowhere near the soldiers. I didn't even know if they were still there. We went back to the kitchen to clean it. The day went as usual, except for fear of crazy soldiers. We worked until we were tired and hit the bed. As I laid there, a smile crossed my face, and I whispered, "I knew you were alive, Daddy."

That night I dreamed of getting that watch I always visited in the village. I needed my security blanket. The next few days were the same with work. Thank goodness there were no more rowdy soldiers – at least not the ones looking for Muslims to kill. The only soldiers coming were the ones that talked about destroying the Muslim parts of Bosnia, which hurt my heart as well. We cleaned the toilets of those dirty people, to keep the hope of surviving. We went on like that, getting a few communications from Dad and the rest of the family. We tried to reach my Njanja but we couldn't. Connections were getting even worse. We just kept hoping and tried to remain calm.

All of this was making me grow up so fast. Occasionally, some kids would come to the hotel, and I would make friends for a few hours. That helped my sanity. I was supposed to go to school soon but, as much as I needed normalcy, I was scared to be on my own with the kids. Then it dawned on me. I had turned eleven. We had completely forgotten my birthday and everyone else's. That's when I realized that celebrating small occasions like birthdays were important. It's the little things that mattered most, and that is when I started focusing on small beautiful things to get me through each day. The days continued as such. We tried every day to reach our family. We had a feeling that the war was worsening and we wanted to know if they were okay. Mom tried twice a day but could not get through. Those were agonizing days; worrying about everyone was very draining.

Chapter Twenty

Another terrible day came on May 13th, when our world crumbled again, especially Mom's. We went into the office to call our family and my grandma Njanja. We finally communicated with my aunt and, just as the operator was losing communication with us, we heard my aunt saying, "Can she hear us?" The operator told her to speak, but it seemed like she couldn't hear us. As we were trying to say to her, we could hear her. She said, "How can I tell her that her mom passed?" We heard her clearly, and Mom fell to her knees. My heart froze. Mom took a minute and then asked how she died. My aunt realized that we heard and started crying as Mom gasped for air. I was stunned and numb as the tears rolled down my face, and my aunt continued, "A week ago, she got hit by shrapnel from a grenade." My heart just dropped as I held Mom's hand. I couldn't believe I lost my Njanja. The whole room looked gloomy and sad. Everyone was devastated. Mom's heart was racing so hard that I could feel the beat in her hands. As much as Mom was trying to comfort me, she continued to talk to my aunt. It had happened near the house. The grenade fell while she was outside, and hit her in several places, including her heart. She didn't die instantly, but a little bit later as they were trying to help her.

She listed a few other neighbors they had lost. Their neighborhood was destroyed, but there was not too much damage to their house. Everyone else in the family was okay. My uncle was trying to get them food, but it wasn't easy. Mom continued to weep and stayed speechless. Silence consumed the room until my aunt said that Njanja, on her death bed, told her to tell my mom that she dreamt of my dad with a haircut – which, in her beliefs, meant that he was going to get rid of a big worry and burden. My whole family believed in those tales and, for just a split second, it made us feel a little better. Mom said her goodbyes and sent her love to the family, as did my aunt. She thanked the operator and, as she cried even harder, squeezed my hand, and brought me closer.

I started crying even harder as she hugged me tightly. I could feel her heart breaking. She hadn't been able to say goodbye to her mom. We lost our Njanja. Another amazing soul lost to the world. I kept telling her, "I'm sorry, Mommy. I'm going to miss her so much." She just kept holding me and crying. The sorrow and feeling of loss were almost too much to bear. We sat there for a bit until we gathered the strength to get up. The manager helped us out and told my mom to take the day off and relax in the room. He said that they would bring food up there. We slowly went to the room and laid down on the bed together, holding each other, and cried ourselves to sleep.

I woke up in the middle of the night, to see Mom with a little lamp on the floor, weeping and praying for my grandma's soul. I looked at her for a moment, then squeezed in next to her – between the beds – and started reciting the prayers that I could remember Njanja taught me. Though her eyes were full of sorrow and tears, I could see that she was happy, I joined her. We prayed together, and then she told me that everything would be okay and to go back to sleep. Sweat ran down my face, mixed with tears. My heart was aching so bad that I felt like it was trying to come out of my chest. The severe hurt made me nauseous. All I could do was keep repeating the prayers.

The next morning, my whole body felt like it had been run over by a truck. Mom was up, doing things to occupy her thoughts – a robot going through the motions. It was like the life has drained out of her. The moment she saw me, however, she smiled. I know that smile now, more than ever – when a child looks at you, and they are the only thing that keeps you going. No matter what's happening, they need you, and you need to be present for them. She came over and hugged me, telling me that we needed to get dressed. She gathered some food for breakfast downstairs. We were going to take this day and go to the village. She was trying to be absolute and go on. She was terrific at that, telling me, "Njanja is in a better place, happier and not suffering. She is watching over us and wants us to live our lives and get through this together. We have to be strong and continue, but remember she is always with us. " I was devastated. My heart was so hurt, I started crying, and I simply responded, "Yes, Mommy."

She hugged me and told me that it was reasonable to mourn to let it out. So, letting it out is what I did. It was such a painful loss. I felt like everything was being taken away from me one thing or person at the time. The feeling of loss and loneliness was so strong that it was poisoning my body. I felt the heavy energy in my heart spreading everywhere, and all I could do is let it. At that point, I couldn't take it anymore, losing so many people. My grandmother's death made me angry and resentful. I needed to let it out. I was screaming inside. I wanted to scream out loud, but a cold chill came over me, letting me know that nobody would help. The surge of emotions was overwhelming. As a young child, losses like that either break you or make you stronger. I couldn't fathom losing anybody else. I wanted Dad with me, and I needed to hug him. We both cried more, and we kept releasing the heaviness. I guess that helped us gain the confidence to be stronger and go on. We gathered ourselves and went to the village. We walked in silence as we watched the birds, the lake, and the nature around us. It was peaceful and calm. We held hands tighter and with more meaning than ever. I didn't want to lose one second with Mom. I know my mom wished the same. There was a calmness in the big beautiful pine trees, and the reflections on the lake – without one ripple in it. I could hear the squirrels running and birds fluttering around me. I felt like I was in another dimension, but I kept walking, hoping Njanja was with us and was bringing us that feeling of serenity.

As we came to the village, we did our usual thing, looking in the stores and wishing to have a dime to buy anything. We enjoyed the little stores and people, the smell of the delicious food cooking. For what it was worth, it helped us to have a little sanity. As we browsed, without even realizing it, we ended up standing in front of the store that had the watch I wanted. Mom signaled for me to go into the store. As I did, Mom pulled out some money to buy it. I looked at her, and she just smiled, I couldn't believe it! I was going to get the watch I wanted! I asked Mom if buying it was okay, and she told me, "We have worked hard. I saved some money, and you deserve it." It was so wonderful to have. To me, it was like winning the lottery – that little inexpensive (yet expensive for us) watch. I hugged her, and that small moment was a bright light in our darkness. I thanked her so many times, and I never took that watch off. Not even to sleep.

Our days continued as they usually did, work, and more work. The worst was enduring the comments and looks of pity from the guests, who were all stuck up and self-loathing, unable to have real compassion for human life. They viewed us, refugees, like dirt. Mom taught me, "They're lowlifes. You should feel bad for them. It should give you pleasure to know that you are more intelligent than they are." It was a hard thing to understand at the time, but it made more sense with every encounter.

It was about two weeks before I had to start school in the adjacent village a few miles away. I was not looking forward to the school or strangers but, by nature, I craved kids and playing with them. I was ready for some normalcy. Meanwhile, we hoped for any word from Dad. I missed him so much. We couldn't get in touch at all, and every day that went by was like a knife stabbing me in my chest. The thought of losing him was so painful. I tried to forget that he was actually with the savages that put us here, and he was being forced to fight and survive on the front lines. The second I let myself think about that, I felt like I wanted to act like a two-year-old having a tantrum. I couldn't take the pain of Dad suffering. It disturbed me. This feeling compounded with the loss of my Njanja was almost too much hurt to bear. However, I needed to stay sane if I was ever going to see my dad again. Honestly, that was what kept me going and hoping. We never stopped trying to contact him. Day after day, we tried calling or looking for messages.

I remember meeting a family that came to vacation for a few days before school. I had no idea how it was possible for anyone to vacation in this state of war, but, up there in the mountains, it was quiet. Nobody was attacking this area, which was only a passage for all the soldiers and murderers. We were on top and the people suffering every day were on the bottom, in the valley. I felt guilty, being up here while the rest of my family was in fear of losing their lives. I used to think of them often, my cousins, aunts, uncles. I often thought of Daniel and Senka. I hoped they were okay, I felt guilty for leaving them, and I prayed for them. All it did was make me sad and hang my head down low. Still, to this day, I never knew if they made it out or not.

That's the sad state I was in when one little girl, and her older sister, noticed me. I was helping run the food to their table. The little girl asked me why I looked so sad. "I am just tired," I replied, with a forced half-smile. I asked her and her family if I could get them anything else, and the mom rudely turned to her daughter, "Don't talk to that refugee! She is probably dirty. Ask for our waitress to bring the rest of our food and drinks." Then she turned to me with a, "Shoo. Shoo!" She was acting like I was an animal, and I just nodded and stepped away as commanded. If I had been holding anything in my hand, it would have ended up on her head.

I've never understood where all this hatred came from, but I always figured it had to be from that continuous propaganda. The news channels kept feeding people lies about who refugees were. For all they knew, we were Serbian. *Why treat your Serbian friends this way?* I guess our accents gave away that we were not from Serbia, but it was such a shameful stigma – that the refugees that were not pure Serbian were not worth it. It was Hitler's mentality all over again. It was Nazism – another holocaust was likely. We had already heard of genocides committed up in the mountains. Mom saw my face after I entered the kitchen, and she knew that the family had hurt me. She forced my eyes to meet hers and told me, "They are the issue. Not you."

Later that day, I saw the girls playing outside. They both ran to me and asked, "Hey, do you want to play with us?" I was shocked and asked if their mom was okay with that. The big sister said, "Don't worry about Mom. She is a little cranky lately." That moment showed me that kids have this innocence and beauty about them. They don't see evil. Kids want to be safe and play. Maybe, just maybe, there was still a chance for our country, if we kids could hold on to our humanity. I smiled and said, "I would love to," and so we played for a bit. It felt good to interact with kids. Although I couldn't stay long, the short playtime was a treat for my soul and mind.

Chapter Twenty-One

Once those girls left, however, there I stayed... and I still felt unfulfilled, longing to hear from Dad. When we finally got through to him, he was not in airport anymore. They had taken him to a Serbian base. That was another painful phone call. I knew something was wrong again when the operator left us a message to reach Dad at the hospital recovery center. Anguish came over me. He was still alive, but he was injured, "Oh my god, I am going to lose my dad too!!!!" My brain was stuck on that feeling. As Mom talked to him, my soul wanted to hear his voice – hear what was happening – but my body just wouldn't move or react. I was hearing their conversation, but all I could feel was my aching heart. Daddy was hit in his leg by the shrapnel of a grenade. *Did he lose a leg? Will he ever walk again?* All these questions flooded my head. I was so scared and confused. All I could hear was the echo of Dad's voice as he explained it all. I could feel his fear.

I listened intently and all I could imagine was this being his last farewell. The numbness spread over my whole body. Dad was short and to the point, because he was a prisoner after all, and was conscious not to say anything he should not. Mom had to read between the lines of a lot of what he was saying. His anger and fear were so strong, even over the phone, but there was also a certain hope and blessing in disguise in his voice as well. I was looking for any positive vibe so I wouldn't pass out. I focused on his voice and being thankful that we were even talking to him. He was still with us. He said that he went through the worst day of his life, if that was even possible after all he had been through. After the grenade shrapnel had hit him, they transported him to the clinic on site. The shrapnel had been laced with cyanide, and he had to hold on tight through antibiotics and primary care and wait for an entire day to see if the poison would spread. If it did, they would have to amputate his leg.

I choked up when I heard that, more tears started rolling from my eyes. Mom's knees locked up when she heard that. She supported herself on the counter. It looked like she got lightheaded. I reacted immediately, holding her, but she recovered quickly. She needed to hear the rest from Dad. She needed to be strong again, "Honey, please repeat the last thing." He said that he was now in the main base hospital and that the leg was still there. Apparently, there was no poison on that shrapnel, or at least not enough to cause damage. He just needed to continue the dose of treatments and to be there for a week or two to make sure he would heal well. Our necks relaxed. He said that he got really lucky. He ran into a longtime friend who was the commander of a main Serbian base. That was why he was able to settle in and be taken care of and not finished off. Nobody wanted wounded prisoners who can't be on the front lines. "Front lines!!!" I exclaimed. Yes, the front lines were where he was spending most of his time. Dad heard my little voice and asked to say hi to me. Mom passed me the phone.

My voice cracked as I said, "HI, Daddy. I'm so happy you are okay. So happy to hear your voice." He told me that he loved me so much, and that he couldn't wait to see us soon. I chuckled and told him I couldn't wait either. Those words didn't sink in at all until way later, but all he said before his goodbye was that there was a letter coming to us. "Bye Daddy." Mom took the phone and told him how much I missed him and that she had been working on reaching out to every possible contact, to see how she could help get us all out of this forsaken country. She mentioned a few names and documents she needed. He said he would work with his commander too. They promised to talk again in a few days to hear his progress with his leg. He told her he loved her very much and to kiss me.

As she hung up, I think Mom had a different tune playing in her head. For the first time, she might have been just a bit optimistic. I liked to see her like that.

God knows we both needed some positivity. We were like hamsters running in a wheel of death. Rotting away in misery. I liked the new energy, but I was confused. After all, we just found out that Dad was injured. We were not quite sure how badly and how it would affect him walking. I was not sure how that was positive. She knew I was confused, so she turned to me and hugged me and said how much I mean to her... and that this situation might be "a blessing in disguise." I really didn't understand what she meant, but I could feel her energy and that was good enough for me. I looked at my wonderful watch and saw 11:11. I thought that was a good number to remember. She hugged me and we continued walking, "Let's go have some ice cream and rest up, because tomorrow you start a new daily routine. School time!"

I choked up immediately, "Wow, school time??" I needed to go over my route to school. I needed to revise my bookbag and all materials. I was thinking of school, instead of surviving or what to eat or where to hide. Is this life turning out differently? I was excited for some normalcy, even if it meant mixing in with Serbian kids. Maybe, as Dad always told me, I was meant to do something great after all. Thinking about it all mentally and physically exhausted me. I thought I would sleep like a baby, but I was mistaken. That was one of those nights where the silence was so uncomfortable. I could not sleep without the sounds of falling grenades.

School time was a very scary idea, but I was ready for something more so I turned my fear into excitement. I got ready in the morning, and Mom had everything ready for me as she escorted me to the bus. I swear I was more nervous at that school bus stop than being around bullets and grenades. Mom had trouble letting go of me, but she knew this was for the best. I could not lose any more school time. As I waved to her, the bus left. I was nervous. I needed to go to the bathroom. I felt like an alien. I thought that everybody knew that I was this horrible refugee and they were giving me the evil eye. It's crazy what a few months of continuous belittling did to my confidence. I calmed down a bit when I remembered that kind act of play from the two sisters at the hotel, and how some kids still have kindness in their hearts. It also helped that all of the kids around were going to same school so I was able to follow them to the right place.

When the stop came, all the kids got out and proceeded to the entrance. I was looking for the main office, where I needed to sign up. The school was very small, so different than schools from Sarajevo. It was very old, and it looked quite primitive, but you could tell it was a school filled with cheer, kids' drawings, and laughter. I started to feel better. I entered the office and asked the lady to sign me in and to get my class schedule. The white-haired lady gave me a look up and down. I could tell she was judging me like everyone else, but she had been in the school system for a long time and still loved and valued teaching and taking care of kids. She took care of me and sent me on my way to class. I walked a very short distance to visit my locker but didn't really have anything to leave there.

As I walked into class, I got a few weird looks. My teacher was a tall, skinny, redhead that smiled at me and told me to sit wherever I liked. I sat at the front of the class, because that is what I always did. I had to remind myself that I was here to learn. The time came for introductions and, as we all went around the room, I spoke my name and where I was from. All I heard was shuffles, mocking laughter, and sighs. I knew I had a long journey ahead of me. That was further confirmed when it was time for lunch.

We were served our lunch and went outside. It was not bad: some meat, veggies, bread and rice. I served myself and started to realize nobody was acknowledging me, let alone saying hi. I knew I would have to sit alone and so I did. A boy stepped up and stood in front of me, "Hey you? Aren't you a little too fat to eat that? Aren't you supposed to be a refugee with no food?" I thought to myself: *Oh boy. Here we go again. I will explode.* I was so full of nerves and anger and tired of nasty people. I lifted my head and looked at him, "You- I..." and then angry tears came down my face. My ego could not let me just run away, so I stood up to him, "If I were you, I would not sleep at night. Because my dad, the Serbian commander, will come and destroy your ungrateful, nasty family." I didn't even know where that came from, or why I would say that, but I did. The boy looked at me and was absolutely sure that I was not joking. That actually resonated with all the kids that were around. He was in shock and didn't know how to answer. He just walked away.

In this volatile state, you never knew who you can mess with. After all, we were in a state of war. Just like that, based on a lie, now I was not known as a refugee, but a daughter of a Serbian commander who was fighting for their Serbian cause. I was not just some weak lowlife refugee. I was at their level, if not higher. I went with it as I saw the mood and energy shift in my favor. The lie was the only game I could play in order to fit into this God-forsaken refugee life. I was interesting all of a sudden. They all just looked, and I continued eating in peace. When we returned to class, I had two girls come up to me, ask what my name was, and make small talk. One of the girls asked if my dad was really a commander. With conviction, I said yes and that I could not say more, as it was a military affair. We talked about school work and partnering up for some book reports that were in our syllabus.

I went home that day to the hotel, where Mom waited for me at the bus stop. She couldn't wait to hug me and, believe me, I couldn't wait to see her. I told her about my day, and she just smiled and said, "Well done. Whatever you need to do in order for nobody to mess with you." For the next few days it continued as such. I couldn't help Mom as much with work, because I dedicated my time to school, but I still was there getting reminded that we were there to serve. I still had weird looks and snobby people thinking I was the scum of the earth.

Even my teacher was biased, never giving me any extra credit or acknowledging my work. Her agenda was clear, to keep Serbians advancing and leave refugees behind, especially if they could get ahead and be better than them. Even the cafeteria lady refused to give me certain foods or lied that there was no more, when clearly other Serbian kids had it on their plates. At recess, kids would throw rocks my way or not allow me to play a certain game. It was very tough but I had no other choice. Thus, I stuck to the story of my dad as a commander and other lies to sustain my sanity and to try to fit in.

The refugee life was incredibly hard. I felt like I was living a double life just to get through the day. I truly was lost. This was the time in my life in which I was supposed to figure myself out – what I liked and didn't – but, instead, I was just doing whatever to fit in. I didn't know who I was, and that shaped me into who I am now, a true chameleon with no strong sense of who I am. All of that taught me a lot, that later would serve me so well. None of that mattered to me then. I was focused on surviving, hearing from Dad, and getting out of this place.

Chapter Twenty-Two

Mom was working on getting us all out of the country. She worked hard, even doing night shifts to pay for those papers. I overheard so many of her phone calls and saw her stacks of applications. The days were hectic and unpredictable. The flight or fight instinct within us lit up all the time. The only constant was that we had each other and the beautiful nature walks we did together around the lake, admiring the trees and animals and stars. In that natural environment, we were allowed to be ourselves, just us. I didn't want to go back into the daily battle – for crying out loud I was still only eleven! I felt like I had the world on my shoulders.

Despite all of this, I was doing very well in school, often having very successful exams. That was yet another reason the other students resented me. I was a *smart* refugee. I liked coming from behind and being better than they were. It gave me a sense of pride, accomplishment, and just a little bit of control. The main goal, of course, was to see Dad. Every day, the minute I came home, I would ask about him. Then, one day, I didn't have to ask Mom about him at all – because she greeted me with a letter from him in her hands! I was so excited. I jumped up and down, grabbed her, and ran to the room to read it.

The letter started; *My dearest angels. I miss you more than the desert misses the rain. I can't wait to hold you in my arms again*. We both started weeping at the same instant. Truth be told, we sobbed through the entire letter. Dad was more of a hero to me now than ever. He went on to explain that he was forced by the TO in Dobrinja to go back to our old neighborhood near the airport, because of the growing tension and his Serbian last name. Reading between the lines, he went so that he wouldn't be murdered in his sleep. He had no place to be or hide. He was all alone. Unfortunately, the Serbians had already overtaken the airport neighborhood and set up perimeters, camps, and mines everywhere to ensure security. He somehow made it into the complex where our house used to be and was hiding in one of the abandoned apartments near where we used to live. He had no water or food, left over opened cans and rock-hard bread were delicacies for him, but it kept him alive. He died a thousand deaths every day.

At night, the soldiers would randomly break into the apartments to make sure no one was hiding. They would break in using SWAT techniques, breaking in the doors and shooting everything in front of them with machine guns. He said that he got lucky the first time they stormed in. Even though he heard them coming and was quick enough to hide, he had been certain that he was going to die as he heard them burst in and start shooting. He said that he knew that was the end. The machine gun shots were deafening. He just hid in a corner and remembered us. As the shooting stopped, he heard the soldiers yell that it was all clear to move forward. He counted his blessings that he was still alive. With the help of higher forces – God, the universe, or whatever he believed in at that moment – he was saved. The soldiers fired the bullets in every direction – making swiss cheese out of the walls. However, he survived because of his position in the corner, the main basement door in front of him covering the entrance door of his basement to where he was and the angle they were shooting from, he was left untouched, a real miracle. He said it felt like he lost twenty-five years off his life from the enormous stress, "*I will tell you more in detail when I see you.*"

I loved reading those words and thought to myself: *When he sees us!!!!!* I smiled in joy. I was sad about what he was going through, but happy to hear he was coming. I wanted to ask questions and jump up in joy, even while still crying over his hardships. He could not speak to us about anything that could endanger him or us. He mentioned that he had to venture out every once in a while, to get food and water. That was a dangerous endeavor, because of all the snipers and Serbian soldiers patrolling the neighborhood. He knew that he needed to escape soon or he would get caught. It was hard enough to survive with no food or water or clothes, but the hardest thing was keeping his mind sane. Sitting alone all day in the basement, counting the minutes until something or someone would kill him. Talking to himself. Planning things out. Keeping his mind off of his thirst and hunger was crippling but reassuring himself of his survival was the hardest.

Your mind starts wandering and playing tricks on you, he mentioned. I knew exactly what he meant. I had seen it in many faces of people in the basements. I felt it myself many times. Those were early symptoms of losing your mind. I couldn't imagine how he survived: *What was he telling himself every day? How had he calculated to escape?* All he had to do all day was daydream and watch outside with caution. He mentioned that the only light in his life, the only thing that made him move forward and focus, was the thought of being with us again. Every day was a battle.

Then the day came that he decided to go out onto the street and act like a Serbian soldier. He knew that was his only chance to pretend, and hopefully get away. He observed the soldiers from the holes in the wall and listened to them when they were close by. He noticed that a lot of the Serbian soldiers had white bandanas around their right arms and a red handkerchief in their pocket. I guess those were the signs of the patrolling Serbs. He gathered his strength and left the apartment, carefully making sure that nobody saw him. He tied a bandana of his own and started acting like one of the soldiers. He walked in the middle of the street, just like all of them did, and made sure that his signs were obvious to the numerous snipers that were probably watching. *What a feeling, knowing that someone has your life in their hand with one pull of the trigger.* His adrenaline is pumping, but he persevered and did exactly what he observed the others do.

Although he had regular clothes, he pretended he was one of the civilian warriors. His heart was beating out of his chest as he walked toward the end of the street, having a plan to continue North in hopes of heading back to Dobrinja or the suburbs in between. As he walked, he heard numerous shots and grenades falling in a distance. Some of the shots were really close. *The bloodstains and smell of the decaying bodies and dogs was unbearable. The destruction made neighborhoods unrecognizable,* he wrote. All of it was surreal, but what took his breath away were the torn bodies lying on the street. He didn't flinch, so as not to cause any attention, but it made him throw up in his mouth.

He heard a commotion on the next street, soldiers drinking and raiding houses. He wanted to avoid any contact, so he nonchalantly kept walking. He entered the alley to check out the other street that would lead to the edge of the neighborhood. Their voices weren't as strong in that direction, so he took a breath and continued moving. The other side of the street, which was closer to the entrance of the airport, was truly a "Code Zero." There was nothing left there, just foundations of buildings, holes and blood. As Dad continued walking, he stayed closer to the buildings... then he noticed a body on the street moving, attempting to crawl.

The body had the same attire and bandana and was asking for help. They were the only ones on the street, so it was hard for Dad to hide from him. As much as he wanted to just continue walking, he had to try to help the person, even if it was a Serbian soldier. He knew that many had met the same fate as him and were forced to be there. He ran and turned the guy around, telling him he would help. To Dad's shock, it was a man he knew, Edad, who immediately recognized him and called him by his nick name, LAZO, which was short for his last name. They were both happy to see each other. They were good friends, back in the day they used to sing opera together and travel. After their singing days had ended, they instead

160

would meet once a week at a local bar and drink and sing for a bit to reminisce about the old days. They kept in touch before the war and couldn't believe they had found each other her and now.

Dad immediately lifted him up, asking what was wrong. Edad's upper thigh had been shot. He couldn't feel it. Dad took a look, and it was hard to do anything about it. He knew that they needed to move out and find a place to get away from the street. Dad put him over his shoulder and carried him. Edad told Dad that he was one of the Serbian managers in their camp, but that he got into the wrong neighborhood. Nobody came to rescue him. Even though Edad has assumed that he was a soldier, Dad told him the truth – that he was hiding. He trusted Edad after all these years. Edad told him not to worry, and that he was considered a soldier so long as he had his ID displaying his Serbian name.

Dad continued assuring himself us that he had the will and the hope he needed to come to us soon, if only he could reach the base. He walked strong but, just as he feared, he came across a few Serbian soldiers that were monitoring barricades. They were brutes looking for blood. They didn't care what soldiers came by. They just wanted trouble. Sure enough, they took Dad and Edad to the camp, where both of them would be judged and, perhaps, killed. *I will talk to you more about my story but I want you to know that now I am okay and that I had no choice but to do what I did. I will speak with you and see you soon. Keep the hope up and always find something beautiful in any situation. Love you always, Bruno.*

We both took a deep breath after that last sentence. I was in shock and nauseous from the rollercoaster of emotions. I usually hated reading, but I poured over this letter again and again. I took Mom's hand and we both sobbed. She said he would be okay, that we would all make it. I couldn't think of anything else for hours. I just dreamed of that moment when we all would make it out together, with my dad. I couldn't believe what he went through and hoped his leg would recover.

I was more at ease, but full of questions that I started asking Mom. She just told me that Dad's injury could be his ticket out, a blessing in disguise. He had a bigger chance of escaping from the base as an honorary soldier. Then it all clicked in my head. Although I was so sad that he got injured, and I could not bear for him to be hurt, that could get him out of the front lines and hopefully to us. He had always told me that there was something good in every situation, and here it was. I know Dad knew a lot of people, and I hoped that his luck would follow him as it had so far. I knew in my heart he would be okay and holding me soon.

Chapter Twenty-Three

That day went on as usual, except I kept smiling as I thought of that letter. There seemed to be more soldier traffic in the hotel that day. Hateful Chetniks always looking to cause trouble, rape, or destroy something. They came in very drunk, destroying chairs and plants. One of them even pulled one of the waitresses toward him, shouting that he wanted to tear her up. She wiggled out of his hold and they just laughed, shouting, "We will kill all Muslims and Croats! If any of them are hiding here, they will be found and run over with a tank." Those threatening scenes always made Mom and I run into our room to hide, hoping they wouldn't find us.

Things were like that in school too. When I took the bus, I would constantly see bombs, machinery, and buses of armed young soldiers heading right toward Sarajevo. My hateful teachers would only talk about how horrifying the Muslims are and how Muslims and Croats were not human. "They are roaches. The soldiers should rape and kill them all." It was hard to hear that and not want to punch everybody every minute, but I had no choice but to shut my mouth and go on. The children would talk the same way and spread the hatred, they talked of "growing up and killing them all." Little did they know that I was one of them. It was a lot to accept for a kid, but I had no choice. I even told Mom I did not want to go to school anymore. I told her that all I am learning in school was hate, and certainly it did not help me grow. Compared to my old school in Sarajevo it was night and day. This world was small and obtuse.

The next few days were awful, but the straw that broke the camel's back was the very last day I went to school. At recess, we heard distant guns firing and bombing that was happening in the city. That alone was enough to give me major anxiety. Those bombs and bullets were falling on my dad and family. What made it worse, however, was that all of the teachers, staff, and kids started celebrating and cheering it on. The teachers even let the kids stay outside longer and skip the next class so that we "could support the bombing and cheer on their victory over Muslims." They actually put on TV the recordings of Serbian conquering, bombings and destroying of the city. The video was awful and made the hairs on the back of my neck stand up the whole time. I was sick to my stomach. The video played the destruction, burning houses, while the soldiers were celebrating. The entire school was cheering on the video.

It felt like I was the only one with any humanity left. I couldn't even watch. I was so uncomfortable and couldn't believe that I was surrounded by such ignorant animals. I just couldn't watch the video. A few bully kids noticed that I was uncomfortable and one of them started asking me, "Why aren't you supporting our soldiers? Are you sure you aren't a Muslim roach too? Is that why you're not cheering?" My explosive nature was bubbling. I was enraged. My ears felt like they would explode, but I knew it was life and death. I grabbed his shirt, tearing it in half, and said, "My Serbian family was killed down there and my dad is fighting there. So, I'm emotional. So back off."

The kid, to my surprise, backed off – even if he was mad about his shirt. The teacher saw it all, and clearly heard what I had said. She paused and said, "We thank your family for fighting for us." Once the bullies heard that, they backed off even more. I nodded at her, and then at everybody else – all a lie in order to keep the peace. The bully growled under his breath, "You disgusting, fat beast. Tearing my shirt." I did not acknowledge him, but those words engraved deep in my heart and soul. He made me feel so low. To this day, those words burn into the core of my insecurities. I was not good enough, I was fat, I was low. I didn't belong anywhere and nobody liked me.

I went home that day and tried to do what Dad told me in the letter: *find something good in every situation to get me through*. Mom was very busy with her grueling work, but she gave me support however she could. She told me to be tough, but it was getting harder to accept our worsening conditions when I knew things could be so much better. Dad's letter came at the right time, talking about timing in life. It really helped me. I asked Mom if I could go to the lake to walk. She said not for too long, and to be back by twilight. So, I went. I could still hear residual firearms in the background, but it was peaceful by the lake. Nobody was there, just nature and I – exactly the way I wanted it: perfect, undisturbed, loving, accepting and pure. I sat on the bench and watched the ripples in the lake as they formed and went away. I wished so much to be somewhere else, anywhere but here, but I wished most for my dad. Before I knew it, twilight came and I was gazing up at the stars again. Those mountain skies are full of the most beautiful pure galaxies and, sure enough, another shooting star just for me. It was so bright and beautiful and I wished for him again, I wished for my dad in my arms and to be gone from this awful place.

I went back to the hotel a bit more relaxed and told Mom what had happened in school and at the lake. Needless to say, we decided that I would not go back to school again, "I have a plan, honey. We will be out of here in no time. I'm working on getting us out of the country to either Australia, Spain, or the USA." This brought a perplexed and scared look to my face, "That is the only way. They are accepting and helping mixed-marriage refugees. They will accept us and help us get on our feet and start a new life. There is no life in this country. We don't belong anywhere." Her words, and the plan, validated my feelings of not belonging. Mom gave me something to look forward to. She explained that, because of the war, the Church World Service and other humanitarian organizations were working on helping refugees who had no place to go. They were relocating them in different countries, where they would be given opportunities and be sponsored. These organizations would provide sponsored visas by the government and an opportunity to work and survive.

I was excited, but scared as well: *another country, another language.* My excitement for travelling and overcame any fear. It also helped that we had travelled so much as a family, so this was going to be our biggest journey yet. Mom has been using her incredible resources, hard work, and will to get her family out, all while she worked washing toilets. She never ceased to amaze me as she fought for us. Needless to say, she inspired me to help as much as I could. I cleaned, washed, and ironed sheets and pillowcases. It was mindless work, but it got us food and a place to stay and some extra money. It was hard at times, mostly because of our egos and the lives we were used to before this struggle. We were a good team, often managing to finish our work early so we could enjoy more free time. I was learning more with her than at that awful school. She told me that soon I would be going to a great school, where I would not miss any more time and would actually learn great things again. For now, she would teach me as much as she could: lessons about architecture, math, and the novels she loved. We would talk about opera, literary characters, and famous artists that I know I would not have learned about in that awful school. We were finally tranquil, and life was as smooth as it could be. I was getting used to this life and was not as stressed. I didn't hear the nastiness as much, unless soldiers came, and we learned to brush off any nasty and arrogant guests that once bothered us. Even the rifle fire had grown more sporadic. I would listen to it at night, just for old times' sake.

Chapter Twenty-Four

After a few weeks went by, we got to talk to the rest of the family. My aunt Mira and cousins were still stuck in their neighborhoods. They had scattered resources, but they were surviving. They were going day by day, but they couldn't get out... and it sounded like they didn't want to. Their homes were intact and their family was around, they were as okay as they could be. On Mom's side, her brothers were okay but, after the loss of Njanja, they were all depressed. I know how they felt. I still felt the depression too. I was thankful that they were okay, however. I noticed that Mom's side of family, which was in a very strict Muslim part of town, were getting somewhat brainwashed to hate all Serbians and Croats. I guess that's what happens in civil wars. Those areas hated Serbian soldiers, with good reason, but they were also hateful and unforgiving of <u>any</u> Serbs, even a Serb like Dad. I could see that the hatred wasn't only on one side. It was widespread across all religions and sects, even among my own family. They cursed the Serbs and called them pigs and were training their youth to hate them as well. My uncle even mentioned that he hoped that Dad wasn't there with the Serbs, turning on his own family. That, if he was, "he was totally dead to them."

I realized that they had pretty much ostracized my dad already, just because his name was Serbian. A man who was in my mom's family for thirty years, who was loved by her side for so long, was suddenly an enemy – even if he hadn't done anything to anyone. My throat dried up quickly. This was truly a war among brothers and it confirmed we did not really have anywhere to go. *Dad was not the enemy*, I thought to myself, *he is just trying to get home*. I closed my heart immediately. The only other thing I heard my uncle say was that we had also lost many distant cousins and neighbors, due to grenades. One of those lost was Kadra, who was killed in her home. I remembered going to her house and eating dinner there. She was a nice older lady. I couldn't believe she was gone. I was very sad to hear that. People were dying everywhere and I could not bear the thought of losing Dad too. The phone call finished and we went on, truly more depressed and heartbroken.

A few days later, we heard from Dad, but he was very short on the phone. He only spoke to Mom, who related the message to me. His injury was okay. He was in a main Serbian base in Pale and had friends in higher positions helping him get a few days out to see family. The week went by, and I kept wondering and dreaming of my dad. I worked with Mom like a slave, but neither of us cared. We were going to be united again. Mom worked hard to get us out of the country, any refugee program and any country that would take us legally and with the right documents. She wrote and spoke to consulates every day, determined to get us out, "Once Dad gets here, we have to get out quick. He can't stay here long." If Dad was found here, they would call him a deserter – and that means instant death. The anxiety was building up, but I knew Mom was determined. We were trying to learn about all of the countries we might end up in, studying them on maps. That was my only education during that period; my hope and sanity while Mom and I cleaned toilets and floors and beds. That work was my hard reality.

I was with Mom when she got papers about applying for residency in Spain and Australia. The thought of being in another country, or even another continent entirely, was mind blowing. She spoke to foreign representatives and used her English knowledge to get a better understanding. She organized and called and did everything she could. I don't know how she did it. She was saving our lives. She used every connection, every phone call she had and person she knew. It was hard, because she didn't have the resources or the money or the place to ask, but she did. Luckily, as the world was watching the tragedy unfold and generations get killed, it was opening its arms to refugees to start a new life, especially those in mixed religion marriages like my family was. We had nowhere to go in Serbian or Muslim lands. I was a half-breed, not belonging anywhere. I had no place in my own country. I was a stranger. I worked and helped Mom as much as I could, playing for maybe just a few minutes outside now and then, or eating ice cream. Most of my "play," however, was with an iron, broom, or mop. Those days were a blur... until, one day, Dad called again.

His voice trembled and sounded very tired and hurt. I couldn't imagine what he had been through, my heart hurt so badly for him. He was alive, however, and he was coming to visit us. He said that Edad, however, didn't make it. He died a day or two after they got to the main base. It was so sad to see him go, but Dad always looked at the positive side of things, "He was my angel. He waited to save me and help me see you guys." Those words were so powerful and helped me learn to always look at the positive aspects of any situation. Mom told him about a few discoveries, but in code, and Dad told her a few things back that I did not understand, but I knew why. Phones were tapped and it was not safe to say everything. We never used our names. When he asked to speak with her, it was using his sister's Serbian name, Mirjana. He told us that he would be here in a week. I almost jumped off the chair. The phone call was quick, but it carried the weight of a thousand pounds of gold. I was finally going to have him back. We were finally going to reunite. I remember what my Njanja told Mom before she went. She had dreamt of my dad and that he was coming home.

The day couldn't come fast enough. Mom worked even harder that week to gather extra money. It seemed like she wouldn't even go to sleep until she found us a place to escape to. She finally got a fax confirmation through Church World Service, a Refugee World Organization, that our family was accepted to go to Spain under a special governmental program to escape the war and have a safe haven. I didn't get all the details. I just remember watching Mom put the fax and confirmation in the big briefcase she had in our room with all of our papers. It was surreal. We were going to Spain! To someplace called Calafell, near Barcelona. I didn't even really have time to absorb it all.

The week dragged on, even with the exciting news that we had a plan of escape. It was scary, because I did not know how the travel would work. *Would it be dangerous and unstable, as all of our other travels were?* I just hoped that there was a better route that protected refugees coming out, that we had the protection of Special Forces. I prayed that it was going to be easier for a change. Mom explained that it should be safer and more organized, via the information coming from the Refugee World Organization, but nobody ever knew in this dirty war.

Chapter Twenty-Five

It seemed like it took forever, but finally we reached the morning of Dad's arrival. Neither one of us had slept at all. We were so excited and nervous, so many emotions. We put on our best clothes and combed my hair like thirty times – more than I probably had in two weeks. Mom looked beautiful, just in a simple dress. We were going to see Dad! He was arriving at one pm, but we were at the bus station by twelve. As we walked to the bus station, I caught a glimpse of the lake behind the hotel. It was bright that day, as if the heavens illuminated our way, and I remembered my wish upon the star over that lake. I don't know if it was just my happy mood – which was rare in those days – but I felt like the whole world, including the lake, was smiling at me. There it was. I will never, ever forget.

There was a red beat up bus approaching. It looked ancient, with racks on the top. I was surprised that it was still working, but it did not matter. It was bringing my dad. I felt like we were in a movie. The bus stopped and all kinds of people were coming out, most looked like regular workers...

... and then there he was. I had to take a double look and the only reason I could confirm it was him was because Mom squeezed my hand. He came out, with only some papers in his hand, and that's it. He wore blue jeans and a torn jean jacket that looked like a bag hanging off of him. His pants were full of holes and scratches. He had lost so much weight that it looked like he was half of the man he used to be. His cheeks were sunken in, with huge bags under his eyes. His skin was gray as a ghost. He smiled when he saw us, revealing a lot of broken teeth. The sadness that came over my body killed me. My heart broke in an instant. Even now, thinking about him in that state makes my heart drop. He walked toward us, limping. He could barely move his wounded leg; the shrapnel had torn it all up.

Once we got closer, I saw the residue of the blood as well. Tears came down my face instantly. My face got super hot and my blood pressure rose.

Everything seemed to happen in slow motion. I noticed every detail, Mom's smile as she walked toward him. Every smell and color of everything around him. I went from walking to running toward him and then leapt into the embrace of his arms. I felt his big heart and love under the bones of his arms and ribs. I was so happy and grateful, but so sad at the same time. We both hugged him. I remembered my dad with big bones, muscular, a handsome big fellow with striking charm. Now he seemed to have disappeared. My heart was breaking, full of both happiness and sorrow, because I could see what he had gone through.

Mom and Dad hugged each other while I sobbed so hard, not letting go of him at all. He squeezed me tighter, and then I heard his voice, "I love you, my pretty girl." I cried even harder – and hugged him even harder too, if that was possible. I managed to say, "I love you too, Daddy." We stayed hugging for what seemed like forever, but I know it was only minutes. I know that he couldn't stand or walk for a while. Once we peeled ourselves off of him, Mom's face was full of tears and make up and my face was just as bad. In that instant, he fell down to his knees and I noticed his red, sunken green eyes were happy to be with us. Tears were rolling down his face. We both got down with him and embraced him even harder. We got under his arms on both sides and helped him walk across the pathway back to the hotel. I don't think we said much to each other on the walk. The tears and silence were doing all the talking.

We were with Dad. I couldn't believe it. People were looking at him strangely, but also with a slight hint of admiration. Not because he had his family around him, but because people thought he was this warrior and soldier that came to visit his family while fighting for his people. I actually saw people treating us better, just on the way to the hotel. They asked if he needed help and said,

"Welcome home, soldier." He had the beard as always, but longer and more untamed than before, like most Serbian soldiers did too. Once we got to the hotel, the manager saw him and welcomed him, telling him what a beautiful family he had and how happy they were to have a soldier visiting them. Mom kept our intentions for escape a secret from everyone.

I still couldn't believe that I was holding my dad. I was so happy. I couldn't wait to ask him a million questions. He grabbed me hard and said, "I'm home, my princess. I will never leave you again." I just started crying even harder and held on to his arm like I was never going to let him go. Mom was sobbing but smiling at the same time. Finally, we got him to the room and sat him down on the bed. This was the beginning of another chapter of our lives. We were lucky to be together and survive so far. Others hadn't: young children, moms, dads, brothers were dead all across the ground of once-beautiful Sarajevo. We were blessed, and we had the most important thing – each other and our lives.

We didn't waste any time once we got to the room. We asked millions of questions and Dad just opened up about everything. We served him cakes and desserts. We had a little coffee maker and Mom served him some. He was so happy to be there. He devoured those desserts, not only out of sheer happiness but also because of lack of food. He took off his jean jacket and we could see how skinny he had become even more. Mom took his leg and lifted it up and he said that it was going to be okay. It was just healing. She put a pillow under it to make him more comfortable. I asked him where he was hurting and he told me a few places, but nothing as major as the leg. Then he stood for a minute and looked at me, "You have gotten so big and beautiful." I just looked at him and started crying again. He shed a tear as well and we hugged again for a long time. I asked him if he had to fight with the enemies and Mom looked at me and said, "Now let Daddy rest and relax. I'm sure we will hear all the stories tomorrow." We just laid there next to him and, as they talked about the few important papers they had, I fell asleep on my dad's chest with a smile on my face.

Chapter Twenty-Six

The next morning, I woke up in my own bed. Mom and Dad were in the other one. Usually Mom would already be at work, but today was special. What a beautiful sight to see them both. I got up and went to snuggle with them. Dad asked me to watch out for his leg, as I was known to be very clumsy, so I was careful as I snuggled next to him. Mom told me that we needed to go, temporarily, to another place to live. We needed to leave the hotel, but they had an empty little house. I asked why, and she said it was because they couldn't afford to accommodate us any longer. Now, with Dad, we needed to be in a more remote place. She said that it would be better and more isolated from the bad people and craziness and only temporary, until we left for Spain.

So, the next day, we packed to leave to the little house. I asked so many questions as we packed – which took no time at all, because we didn't have much to take. I asked Dad about Grandpa Ratko, and he told me that he wished he had seen him more. He told me that, someday, we would go back and see his grave. He missed him. I asked about our neighbors and the people we left behind. He said it was hard to know who escaped and who was killed. I asked him about the rest of the family, and he paused. I knew that something wasn't right. He said that Mom's family thought of him as an enemy now, shooting at them. They didn't understand that he was forced to be in the Serbian army. Dad had to do it or they would have killed him. He said it saddened him to think that his family of many years would think that of him. I hugged him and said that I was glad to hear that he didn't harm anyone and tried not to be on that hateful Serbian side. He hugged me and said that he never wanted to hurt anyone. That he just tried to keep himself alive. Dad hoped that his Muslim family – my mom's family – would one day understand that.

Mom looked at him, heartbroken. She knew well that was the case , having spoken to her brothers and family. She knew that they were turning against him. They were so brainwashed that that's what they believed. I felt even more alone, knowing that we had nothing left back in Sarajevo. Not even part of our family. Now I know why Mom's mission was so clear. We had to get out quick.

We walked to the houses, about thirty minutes from the hotel. These secluded cottages were deep in the hills behind the hotel. Dad limped and rested as much as he could. As we distanced ourselves from the hotel, I looked back and saw it looking so pretty – one of many homes I had in this life. We went through the streets, and then had to climb a bit through the woods. There were hiking paths, so it was not as rough and actually had some places to sit down and rest. The woods were majestic and the temperature was wonderful. The walk was refreshing to me. The breeze was perfect and cooled us off without getting us too cold. The secluded woods offered a tranquility that definitely made it seem like we were going somewhere safer: *our new home.*

As we got deeper into the woods, we saw a few houses in the distance and, just before them, a few scattered little cottages. Mom pointed to the closest one and we continued on strong to get there. It was abandoned and run down. The wood was broken on each side, part of the roof hung down. It had not been used in years. This was going to be our house for the next few days. It had small windows and some were covered with wood. Even with its broken look, it still had a cottage charm. Inside, it was bare. A kitchen with missing appliances. A small bare lightbulb in the bedroom and another in the bathroom. There were a few bricks and plywood and set up as a table. There was no heating or cooling; it was just the bare mountain air. Bricks and plywood had been set up as three beds, "Is this where we are sleeping?" She looked at me with sadness and hurt in her eyes, but she answered the best she could, "Yes, honey. I will make it super comfy for you, you'll see. Plus, it's good for your posture." We laughed. I guess we were refugees after all, lucky to be alive and to have a roof over our head.

As we started settling in, Mom had a woman come over, an older refugee I had never seen before. She was small and shy and brought us sheets, blankets, and comforters. The woman kissed and hugged Mom and told her thank you and left. Mom thanked her as well. It was confusing. I didn't know how she had gotten the blankets, but I guess she had her ways. Both Dad and I looked at her. He sat down on the so-called table to rest his leg as Mom explained. She told us that she knew that woman from the hotel. She works there as well. Mom had given her some money to send to her family. Apparently, that had saved her husband. I guess now that goodness was paying off.

Dad and I started putting some of the sheets over the windows to give us a bit of privacy. Meanwhile, Mom made the beds, fluffing them up with comforters, blankets, and pillows. Sure enough, it looked so cozy. She had done it again. We sat on the beds and it was comfy, Dad couldn't wait to put his leg up and rest. Mom put out the cookies she had carried so we could have a snack. She had some more unpacking to do, but Dad asked her to sit next to us and rest. She came over and we took a second in our cozy little bare cottage to sit down together and hug and reflect on our new life. I asked Dad to finally tell me everything. *How did it go when you went to the base? How did you manage? What exactly happened?* Mom looked at me, "Are you sure you want to bother Dad with this?" I had to, and Dad was very eager to tell me. He got comfortable in the bed and started his story.

"Do you remember when I told you that, when you left Dobrinja, TO started treating me really bad? I couldn't even sleep at night. The tension was too high. I thought they would murder me at any point. I had to escape. I needed to go. My intention was to go up North to stay with my sister, but it would have been a harder task and a lot further, and I had to go and see if I could find anyone else and salvage anything from our neighborhood that I could. I was hoping to find Senka and Daniel or anyone else but also, I also hoped that if I did not it was because they escaped safely. Little did I know that, by going back, all that was there was death, the end. I would be stuck again – this time in an apartment only a few blocks away from where our old house once stood. I went with the car back into the neighborhood. I don't even remember how I made it back without them blowing me up. Once I got there, I knew immediately that there was nothing there but death. I hid and hoped that they wouldn't find me. With the way the perimeters were set up and all the soldiers running around, I was surprised that they didn't see me coming in or capture me right away."

"Once I came into the neighborhood, I realized how lucky I was that they didn't shoot me or torture me. The hardest part for me was being stuck there, just waiting. Knowing that there was no way out. With the lack of food and sleep, your mind starts going crazy. I was talking to myself a lot and trying to reason. I thought I was going crazy many times." I squeezed his hand. We were both in tears. "The only thing that kept me going was the memory of you guys. I needed to see you again. I spoke to you and Mom in my mind and ate grass pretty much. I knew I had to get out as soon as possible. As you know, I got lucky when they were guerilla cleaning the neighborhood. I could have been killed."

The way he was describing it, I could picture it all better than in the letter he wrote. It really hit home how hard that was. I was heartbroken, but we continued intently listening. He hugged us and continued, "I was meant to be with you again. I love you, my girls. I stayed put that night, without moving a muscle. They were burning other houses. I could smell the smoke and just waited for my hiding place to be set on fire as well. I knew it was coming and I knew I had to do something. That night I don't remember eating or drinking anything. I only had one more bite of dry beef and a few sips of water left. It was a hard thing to swallow. I knew that, if I left, the chances of survival were slim, but a lot bigger than staying. I had to gather my strength, and the only way to do that was by talking to myself. I laughed and cried and got strong, slapping myself for doing all of this. I was losing my mind. I was shifting into a weird dimension in my brain. I was giving up. Then, just when I wanted to kill myself and get it over with, your little face came into my mind... and your mom's. You were telling me to go on and to escape. " I couldn't stop crying as I was listening to him, it was the most intense story. I could not imagine being alone like that, trapped to die. My father was so strong, "Please tell me more, Daddy." He continued, as a tear ran down his cheek, "That's when I found Edad, but you know that story already. Edad protected me physically form bullets as I carried him and he was my ticket out because he was placed there to get me out of our neighborhood. I felt bad using him as a shield but I needed to survive and in turn I was trying to help him as well. I used him as a decoy to get into the base hoping to pretend my way in. He truly saved me and he I believe gave his life doing so."

I asked him about the time he spent on the Serbian front lines when they captured him, "That was the worst part, but I was trying to be smart about it. All the captured people were either deserters or, like me, people that had Muslim or Croatian wives and families and were lying about their identity. Most of them were unlucky to lose their families, so their lives didn't have much meaning. Others were young and stupid and wanted to hold a gun and experience being a man with the power of guns. Those are the kids that I encouraged to go in front of me on the front lines so that they would shield me. I tried to reason with them and tell them this was not a joke, but they would not listen, so they went ahead anyways.

They didn't know what a nasty war it was. It was brutal. The first day we went to the front lines, we were in Dobrinja – right in front of the neighborhood where I knew TO was and where we were. We had to go through the dug out canals and start a fight at night or at dusk. So, I usually would let everyone go in front of me as I pretended to walk slow. Then I hid behind a tree or deep in the canal and listened to the massacre that was happening.

A few older, wiser guys would stay back with me. We would just hide or cover each other, as we knew we were on the same page. We were too old and wise to die this way. I armed myself with guns, rifles and bombs, but only for self-protection. I never once shot at the enemy unless they were shooting at me. I hid as much as I could. A few times it was just a few of us, because the nasty commanders would just feel like torturing a few of us by sending us out on missions. One night it was just five of us, and I had to stay closer. We were in the bunkers and had to gain ground. I stayed behind a dumpster and needed to cross over. I let two of them ahead, but then I had to go too. We had to cross this area that was full of TO. At that point I did not have a choice, I crossed over and waited. Then I heard TO soldiers yelling and coming right for me. All I could do was turn sideways and crawl under the dumpster. I threw one bomb after another in their direction so they wouldn't come kill me. I heard the hand grenades go off. All of them were screaming, but none of them made it to me. I had to do it, it was either me or them." He was tortured to say this – and I was too – but I reassured him that, yes, this was a dirty war. He had no choice.

He was looking for forgiveness. I can't imagine what a great burden that was. One that he would always carry with him, but he had to do it. He squeezed my hand and shed another tear. Both Mom and I told him the same thing. None of this was his fault. He did exactly what anybody would have in that situation. He nodded, and I felt his relief, " I remember once, on those front lines, we all went out to try to conquer another TO area. We were in the bunkers and getting killed one by one, our position was weak and TO had placed mines everywhere. Most of us died that day. As they were running, they were getting killed by the mines going off one by one. I saw how dangerous it was, so I stayed behind, looking for anywhere to hide. Eventually, I was able to jump and escape into a sewer opening. I went inside, and it was hell in there. It smelled terrible and it was wet and nasty, but it saved my life from mines. I hid, with the cover of the sewer on top of me. I heard horrible screams, mines going off and bullets. The ground was shaking and it was horrible. I held the sewer top as long as I could. When my arms couldn't hold it any longer, I placed my jacket under it, so it would not lock as I rested my arms. I curled myself into a ball, trying not to touch the nasty sewage, waiting while total destruction was happening outside. I was one of the few that survived that day on the front lines."

"I waited for hours in that sewer. I might have dozed off for a bit, out of pure exhaustion. I stayed until I didn't hear any more commotion. My back and neck were on fire. I couldn't feel them at all, but I had to get out. It was dusk and I slowly moved the cover and lifted my rifle up, just in case a sniper was watching me. Sure enough, I heard a shot. A sniper hit my rifle. I quickly put it down and I tried again a few minutes later. I put my rifle out, with my jacket on it. Again, the sniper, with just one shot, warned me again. This time, however, he didn't hit the jacket or the rifle. I tried moving the cover of the sewer a little more. This time, I heard the *ping* of a bullet hitting the metal cover. At this point I knew that they were toying with me. I put my finger up with my rifle and they fired another shot – another miss. In this war, snipers get paid by kills and bullets, not by missing. They should have already killed me. Why hadn't they?"

"Then it dawned on me. It was Rade from Dobrinja. He was a great sniper, and he had been watching me. I never confirmed it but, in my heart, I knew it was him. He lived in the North part of Dobrinja. I used to visit him, but we stopped hanging out at the onset of the war because he started to be a hardcore Muslim. We knew each other for so long, though. We were really good with each other. He was an Olympic-level shooter, so I am sure TO paid him top dollar. I knew, that he was testing me, that it was someone that knew me and was letting me live. I put my camel cigarettes on top of the rifle and, again, no shot. I put my jacket up and no shot. I moved the cover and, sure enough, a direct hit on the cover again. I put my cigarettes up and no shot. Now I knew that it was him, or someone I knew. I couldn't toy with my life, however, so I decided to stay in the sewer for the night. I smiled, remembering my dear friend and how – even in this life and death situation – he had found a way to mess with me. I was near death but I found a way to smile."

"I guess I dozed off but, when I woke, I knew it was my chance. I opened the cover, put my rifle up, my jacket and… nothing. I again put my rifle a little higher. Nothing. I took a few minutes, gathered my thoughts, and decided to get out and run into the canal, backwards from where I came from the day before. I barely got out of the sewer, because I was in an awkward position. I had lost feeling in my legs and my back was throbbing. I got out and crawled into the dug out canal. I couldn't really see much, but I went by memory. I could hear distant gunshots and grenade detonations, but nothing too close. It was a strange night. The stars were almost coming out of the clouds. It was unusual – the sky was usually filled with smoke – but, that night, the stars illuminated my way. I crawled on my hands and knees in the canal. I heard a shot or two above my head, not sure if it was the sniper or just random shots, but I kept my head down and crawled like an animal as fast as I could."

"I finally reached the opening of the building, where we had a tunnel to our base. I saw our barricades in the distance. It seemed so close, but I had to crawl for a few more minutes. The most dangerous part was approaching the barricade

---

without getting killed by my own side, thinking I was an intruder." Dad wrung his hands. I truly felt like I was there with him, experiencing the fear and anxiety, "At that moment, I remembered that we all had the yellow, red and black armbands that we had to wear as the first line soldiers. They all knew that sign and that gave me some comfort. I just hoped they saw the band in time. The only thing that would help, once I got close, were the strong lights from the tanks and lanterns. My heart was pounding. Yet again I was faced with death. I was more scared than when I was in the sewer. In the sewer, at least I knew my friend would not kill me. Here, they would, even if I was considered theirs."

"I slowly approached, as close to the barricade as I could. I slowly lifted my rifle, with the band tied to it, and shouted, 'Don't shoot! It's me! Lazarevic front line!' Three guards pointed their rifles as I got up on my feet and waved the arm bandana. They aimed at me and quickly realized I was their soldier. They yelled to stay down, and I did, continuing to yell, 'I'm Lazarevic soldier front line!' They told me to walk slowly with my hands in the air. As I approached, they asked me for ID. Once I was secured, they gave me back my rifle and bandana. They questioned why I was alone, so I explained what happened. Of course, I exaggerated that I was the hero, taking care of the few TO people. They brought me inside and put me through the tunnel to the safer path on the other side of the barrier. Once I got in, I proceeded to the campsite where my brigade was. At least half of them were missing, but the few that survived were surprised and happy to see me. They yelled that they thought I was a dead man. 'How did you survive, where were you?' they kept asking. 'How did you make it out alive, with all the snipers and the brigades there?' I told them a grand story of how I killed a few TO and fought for survival. Lie after lie. The commander walked in, saw me, and said that I was a lucky, tough old bird. He patted me on the back and said to come into his office. Everybody was cheering for me but, little did they know that I was just plain lucky to make it. I had made myself look heroic so that, maybe – just maybe – they would get me off the front lines so I could find a way to escape to you guys. I walked into the commander's office and I talked to him about how I had 'slain a few balije.' That they were going to enter into our base if it wasn't for me. The lies were just flowing out of my mouth, but I guess that's what we have to do in order to survive, that's what war makes us: liars, cheaters and murderers."

Dad shed more tears out of sheer guilt and disgust, we both hugged him and told him that we both knew who he really was. That none of that was the real truth. I told him that he was just trying to survive. He was trying to come home to us. We all cried like babies and got closer that evening. I even told Dad about the lies that I had told too, "I said at school that you were a Serbian commander that who come and beat up my bullies... and it worked!" Dad laughed at this, but Mom said, "That's enough, honey. No more stories for today. We need to rest. Soon, we'll need to walk to the refugee camp, where they will be serving dinner."

I didn't want to separate myself from Dad. I held him tight. She let us snuggle while Mom was trying to wash the three pairs of clothes that we all collectively had and hang them up to dry. She was always strong when it came to emotional moments. She cried and held our hands, but she also knew she had to hold us all together, especially Dad now as well. She kissed our foreheads and said, "You two can hold hands all night long, but let's wash up and get ready for dinner." I still could not believe that Dad went through all that he had told us... and he had just started his story. I knew that he was carrying huge guilt inside him, and God knows how much emotional distress. Deep in thought, I washed off in the little running water pipe that was coming out of the wall in the kitchen. The bathroom had a toilet, but not a full shower. I had no idea how we would shower properly.

I washed as best as I could, then we left our cottage and started walking to a tent that was about a five-minute walk toward the northern part of the forest. Dad had a hard time, but he insisted that he had to walk. We came up a little hill and saw a white tent. It sure seemed closer than it was. Dad limped but we helped him eventually make it. It was a small tent, and inside were a few picnic tables, chairs, and what looked like a small kitchen with burners. That's where two ladies were serving hot bean soup and bread. There were not many people, only a few that looked like military families and refugees. Mom whispered that this was part of the worker's village, where workers of Zlatibor and their families lived. You could tell that it was safe, just a bunch of poor people trying to make it.

Mom waved to a few ladies, and they smiled back, so that made us feel more comforting. The beans looked rather unappetizing, but that's what we had so that's what we ate. People at least looked at us differently, especially since dad was a war soldier. They were all fond of soldiers protecting and fighting for them. It was truly a refugee meal in a rugged old place in the middle of the woods. I felt strange there, but I knew we were only going to stay for a week or so. Mom got up and asked for another container to go. She had a little bowl from the room and asked the old lady to please fill it and give us a few pieces of bread. The lady was nice and gave us a bit extra. I helped Dad up and we left humbly, while people just nodded and saluted us.

We walked back through the woods, trying to make it quickly, before night fell and we weren't able to see a thing. It was already sunset, and the mountains were beautiful, with green pine trees and the sky yellowish blue and purple. We started hearing distant grenades. I hugged Dad and said how the grenades scared me and that I couldn't wait to get out. He squeezed me and said we would be out soon, "I only have ten days before they are waiting for me to return back to base in Sarajevo. I promise we will get out before that." I asked him to explain to me what exactly happened, and why they didn't let him go completely. He said that he would explain how it all went down over breakfast. He was tired and we all needed to get some rest when we got back to the cottage.

We walked in and secured the cottage with a chair under the knob, just in case. We all got ready for bed in the very dim light from our one lightbulb. It was a little surreal. I was in a strange cottage in the middle of the mountains, occupied by the Serbians, with both of my parents. I saw my parents settled in their bed, or whatever you would call the brick contraptions we slept on. Then Mom turned off the little lightbulb. There was natural light coming in from the moon and the stars, that beauty that I always loved and connected with. I closed my eyes and fell asleep quickly. My dreams that night were so vivid and so real that I woke up in the morning drenched in sweat, even though it was chilly in the room. Mom was making coffee on the little electric stove she brought from the hotel. She also had water, the bread from the tent, and a few pieces of smoked meat and cheese.

Dad was sitting at the wood table on a chair of bricks, sipping his coffee. I sat up with a smile and jumped on top of him. He hugged me as Mom brought a little plate of sugar for their coffee and we sat down as a family to eat breakfast in a peaceful mountain morning. They asked me how I slept and I told them about my vivid dreams. Mom said that she had them too, so she asked me to share mine.

I told her that I had a dream that the three of us were in an empty meadow, and the grass was dry and yellow. We knew a disaster was coming. A bunch of people were there. Nobody I recognized. Then, all of a sudden, we heard helicopters and soldiers with rifles, bazookas and grenades. They killed everyone and everything in sight. In the dream, we had jumped into a white old school rustic tub with a shower curtain, like from the old days. It was strange. A white tub in the middle of a big empty field, but there it was, and it saved us. We hid in the tub and everything was gone, I guess everyone was killed and we were the only survivors. Little did I know that I would continue to have the same dream almost every week until I came to America, never knowing the meaning. That was the first of many. Both of them looked at me and Mom said, "Well, yes. We will be saved soon and will have the kind of normal life that some people are not lucky enough to have." I thought about the possibilities in our new adventure. Dad held me and said, "You are safe now." Mom prepared a new bandage and gauze for his leg. It looked pretty bad. The wound was semi-closed, but with no blood. It just looked like it was healing very slowly. Dad said that it was okay, and much better than it was before.

Then I asked him how it had happened, and he told me this story, "Well, it was the morning after the sewer incident. They gave me a bit of a leeway. My commander was impressed by my story, so I convinced him to let me be one of the leading officers of the "second or third cleaning crews," as they called them. Those are the groups that come in after the front liners and foot soldiers, once it was a little safer. I convinced him to include me and the other three older guys from my brigade, telling him that we were better in the back when it came to the strategy of cleaning and conquering. The younger guys were better for front lines. He sent me to the base's main general to get his signature as well. I had good luck on my side and the universe keeping me safe again, because the general was a friend of mine – Zoran, from the chorus way back.

I didn't recognize him at first, because he had a long beard and mustache. We hugged and he was happy to see me in the Army, demanding that we have a few cognac shots and tapas to catch up. We were like brothers in that chorus, so it was refreshing to catch up with him. I wished the circumstances were different – and that he was not a general of killers – but, I'm glad he was there, because it saved me. I counted my blessings again, for having the luck to know people at the right time. Needless to say, he signed me and my friends up for the third brigade clean-up crew. He's the same general that let me come here and visit you. So, one day, we were going in after the second crew, in order to loot and clean up the conquered areas. I had a team of six guys. We were all a little older except for one younger guy. All in similar situations, with wives and families in Belgrade or the outskirts of Bosnia. They were all very eager to stay alive and go make it back just like me.

It was dusk. We went into a few houses on the outskirts of Dobrinja and, once we were done, we settled in one house – that was full of food and liquor – to stop and rest. We laid low for the most part. The shooting and grenades were mostly in the distance. We were closer to Serbian-held territory. I didn't want to do any of this, but it was better than on the front lines. Those Serbian Chetniks were brutal. I hated being with them every second, but I had no choice. It was either that or being killed by either side." We nodded and assured him that we understood, "I was angry at first, because I did not understand. But now I know you had to survive. I love you, Daddy. You are my hero."

His voice cracked, and he said he loved us both. Then he shook it off and continued, "While we rested in the house, I went out on a small side balcony to smoke a cigarette. Night had fallen, and I took a deep breath as I ate a little can of beans and took one drag of my cigarette. The other guys were inside, shouting out to me that they had found some Sljivovica, a very strong liquor. As I took another drag, I heard that train sound. That twirling wind sound, and there it was: the huge boom. The detonation knocked me down into the house and shook the whole area. The walls were shattering, things were falling everywhere, the walls in the front of the house were falling and all I remember is lying down with no sound in my ears. I saw the guys pulling me into the house. They were uninjured. I didn't feel my body at all. The guys pulled me in as I watched them upside down. The detonations stopped and it got a little calmer, they were all surrounding me on their knees. I finally got my hearing back and I could hear them asking if I was okay. I saw them looking at my leg, and that's when I saw it: I had a crater-size hole in the middle of my thigh, but not an ounce of blood was coming out."

"The hole was two inches deep, completely seared to the bone. I didn't feel anything. It was very strange, but I knew it was shrapnel from a grenade that got me. I squeezed my leg as hard as I could. They were helping me up, and that's when the blood started gushing out and the pain started. The most terrible pain I have ever experienced. Thanks goodness for the guys that were there. They took their jackets off and tied the wound up as much as they could. They were trying to clean and help me, as well as cleaning the shrapnel and glass out of their bodies. I felt like I had a million little pieces of shrapnel in my face and all over the rest of the body. As the pain increased, the blood was gushing and I passed out. The next thing I remember was waking up in the base camp medical tent."

"I was so grateful for those guys for getting me to the medical center. I never saw some of them again, but I wish them all the best. I probably saved them too, by putting them in that clean-up group, otherwise the front lines may have killed them. I hope they are all with their families like I am today." I squeezed Dad's hand as tears rolled down my face, "As I laid in the hospital, the doctor told me that I was very lucky that I did not get hit higher, as that would have shattered my pelvis and I would have died. It was a huge hit, and even luckier because it only hit soft tissue, not damaging the muscle or any major nerves. He gave me pain meds and penicillin, but also said that the TO grenades were laced with poison. If there was poison in the leg, and gangrene appeared, they would have to amputate my leg. That hit me like a ton of bricks. I was sure that I was going to lose my leg."

I hugged him with all my heart and my soul felt his pain. Mom came over and hugged us both. She was filling out travel papers as he continued, "It was tough, my love. I really thought the worst would happen. Just waiting to see the red line of gangrene emerge to take my whole leg forever. A part of me was thankful that I was still alive, but the other part was full of fear, anger, and resentment. I asked the general to bring me a full glass of cognac and Sljivovica. Since he was an old friend, he sent in my crew with some booze. Before I knew it, I had the two older guys from my brigade come by with a whole bottle of Sljivovica. We started drinking to ease my pain. They tried to make jokes to take my mind off the misery, and it worked. We joked about everything and everybody. We were getting really drunk and, as we finished the first bottle, the general brought in some cognac and drank with us. It was strange for the guys to see that he and I were such good friends. Eventually, the general left and urged all the other guys to get back to their base."

"Then, again, I was left alone. I was liquored up, so the physical pain was subdued, but I was alone. I couldn't take the agony of waiting. So, I drank the rest of the bottle. Don't ever drink like that, Manja. It's terrible for you. I eventually passed out, and the next thing I remember was a nurse waking me up. It was very late in the morning, and she said three words that gave me a new outlook to life, "You are safe," I immediately snapped into reality and looked down at my leg. I saw no red line, no green line, no abnormal swelling. I asked her again, to reassure myself, and she said, "You made it. It's not poisoned. It looks just fine. I will have the doctor come by and take a look. Then I will change the bandage. The doctor couldn't come fast enough. He took a good look, lifted and pulled it, swabbed it to test it... then he smiled and said that I was all clear. I just needed a new tight bandage and a treatment of antibiotics. This bandage would last a few days and he said, 'the drug supply would last my whole trip.' "

"I stared at the doctor, not sure what he was saying. I stayed quiet, of course, and they got me up to walk and took me to the general's office. I limped there as best as I could. Once I entered his office, he greeted me with a hug and laughed, telling me I still smelled like alcohol. He told me that he would give me a vacation break of fourteen days to rest the leg and go see my family as I had asked of him last night. I guess, in my drunkenness, I must have asked again. I know that, talking to him, I had asked before about coming to see you. He handed me the official paper release with dates and travel documents to come here and go back. He said, 'Go see your family and recover. Then come back. I need a strong man and a friend back here at the base to clean up the mess.' I looked at him and thanked him and hugged him. I told him how proudly I would come back, and that I would never forget this. That it meant so much to me to see my family. I had to emphasize that I meant my Serbian family in Belgrade. If they knew I had a Muslim wife and a mixed child..."

He brushed aside all thoughts of possible tragedies, focusing on the salvation that brought him here, "I asked him for an army car, and a sign off for gasoline. He handed me all the papers and documents and we shook hands. He said, 'Now go, and I better see you back here or you are a dead man.' I looked him in the eyes, shook his hand, and said 'yes.' I was breaking every possible honor and value I had but, again, this is war! I asked about safe passages and tunnels and he gave me an all access pass and routes to go. The base was connected directly with Serbia. It seemed like it would be an easy trip. I would drive all the way to the Ljubovica bus station and take the bus to Zlatibor. Again, I had angels lifting me up and helping me through. I was meant to come see you. I was fortunate again. Just like I kept telling you, my little one. You are meant for something bigger than this."

I could tell he was getting exhausted, talking about all of this. I was growing tired just listening. It was such an emotional subject, and yet exhilarating. Mom said to give it a rest for a bit. She needed to talk to Dad about some paper details. I hugged Dad twenty more times and kissed him, "Daddy, you are my hero. I love you!!" He hugged me back hard as he tickled me. Just like old times. Our surroundings were so alien, but the three of us, together, started to feel beautifully familiar again.

Chapter Twenty-Seven

That day, Mom asked if I wanted to play outside around the cottage. I actually was looking forward to it and went right outside. They could see me from the window and I felt safe, so I played with leaves, making "leaf cakes" and "leaf soup." I ran around the hill. I picked flowers and just enjoyed nature, like I always did. The pine trees were so amazing and the crisp air was magnificent.

I made friends with another refugee girl that lived there. She was a bit younger than me, but I didn't care. I had someone to play with! We ran up and down the hill, completely running out of breath and laughing until we couldn't breathe anymore. We collected branches to make little nests. I didn't play too long, but I remember feeling like a normal kid, having a little bit of a normal childhood playing in the woods. For a moment, the war didn't exist. I remember Mom looking out at me from the window and calling me in at dusk, when we needed to go to the tent for food. I went in and took "a refugee shower," as I called it, and got ready to get food again.

Almost a week passed like that. I would speak with Dad. He would do paperwork with Mom and hang clothes to dry in the woods and, of course, I played with my little friend. We would climb and play outside and I loved it. I was happy, for what it was. Mom would tell me to fetch food from the tent because, by that point, they all knew us. Nobody ever passed us by and the cafeteria lady liked me and always gave me more food to bring home. The passage was safe and tranquil. Mom figured it was safe. She could see most of the way to the tent from the window, and the people there were all nice and were not looking for any trouble. I would run quick and come back. Sometimes I was scared and looked for bears – or anybody else to snatch me – but there was always tranquility.

Until, one day, we heard loud banging on the doors of a close-by cottage. Mom and Dad got up and rushed to the door. We saw, through the window, that it was Serbian soldiers looking for someone. They were banging on everyone's door. Dad opened the door when they knocked at ours. My heart was in my throat. I was so afraid that I almost threw up. I was afraid for my dad, scared that they were looking for him. I realized we still had a few days left on his papers, but God knows there were no rules in the war. They were surprised to see Dad. Of course, he played the part of the higher officer. He told them to be quick, as they were interrupting a commander's rest time. They asked for some lady and Dad quickly got rid of them. He closed the door and I think we all got our color back.

We saw them going to the next cottage and we saw them pulling a woman out of the cottage by the arm. She was resisting and had a small child with her. It was terrifying to see that. I was totally heartbroken. I don't know why they were looking for her, but it was not for good, that was for sure. It looked like they were looking for a prisoner. Just like that, they took her – with the little child – and they were terribly rough with her. Her face was full of tears and horror and the little child was terrified too. We just stood there in agony. I was so sad to see that. It was war. I just sat in my little bed and started to read one of my books. I could not take the horror anymore. I had to distract my mind. I did not want to think or analyze anymore, and I had Dad there to protect us. I was still scared.

That night, Dad was like a guard. I was not allowed to go anywhere and we didn't even go get food at the tent, just in case. We stood there in caution. We were nervous but, there was no additional commotion. So, I went to sleep, though I'm not sure Dad did. That same night, I was woken up by a very strong storm. The storms were brutal there in the mountains. The echoes make it a hundred times more powerful and loud. The rain sounded worse than the grenades. I will never forget that night. It rained so hard that it continued into the day. We listened to the rain in the morning. It was even more scary, after the day we had with the nasty soldiers taking women and children to goodness knows where. I remember lightning hitting a tree that was thirty feet from the house, splitting it right in half, leaving the tree bright red and falling on the other side. Thankfully, it fell *away* from our cottage. It's incredible to think of how nature is <u>still</u> more powerful than any war or man-made disaster. It was insane, that lightning scared me more than the grenades we still heard in the background. We stood there, mesmerized, and then ran out to see where it landed. It just lay there across the middle of the forest. A few neighbors came out and they were not fazed. I guess that type of thing happens all the time in the mountains. For us, however, it was the icing on the cake of a terrifying day. We counted our blessings and went on, knowing that only four days remained before we left. Those four days seemed like a year.

We continued our days in the cottage, Mom having to wash our clothes in the sink. She had to borrow some clothes from the hotel for Dad because he literally came with only what he had on. The nights were heavy with gunfire and grenades. We heard helicopters and planes fly over; those would scare us to death. The gunshots sometimes got closer than normal. Those were, most likely, drunk soldiers or some secret shooting deep in the woods. Some of those shootings we heard in the woods were the massacres of innocent prisoners. Those mountains have hidden so many murders. Dad said that they would send any soldiers they wanted killed up into the woods to assassinate them. At this point, I thought, they might be doing it with women and children as well, if the way we saw those soldiers take that lady was any measure.

I could not be outside or be anywhere too far from my parents. Things were getting worse, even in the woods. I was petrified, and relieved we only had two days left. The grenades would still detonate so close that you could feel the earth shaking. It hurt, because they were destroying my town of Sarajevo, my family. Sometimes I would wake up at night, searching for the sounds, and I would hear my dad crying and dreaming vividly. I felt so bad, because I knew that he was deeply scarred. It was tough to see him squirm on that plank of a bed, and then wake up in tears and sweat. I wanted to rush over and hug him, but I wasn't sure if that was the best thing to do. So, I would just whisper to him, "I love you, Daddy." I'm not sure if he heard me, but he would always stop after I said that, so I wanted to believe that my words did help him. Those were our nights at the little cottage.

Chapter Twenty-Eight

The day before our departure to Belgrade, from where we would leave for Spain, Dad had to go see the doctor to make sure his leg was okay. We all went to this little local doctor by the hotel in Zlatibor. Of course, we were treated like gold, everyone somehow assumed that my dad was this high-end commander who was injured in the battle, so everyone catered to him. I guess he looked like a mean soldier, with his beard and stature. The doctor even gave me a piece of candy. We were surprised because, otherwise, we would be treated like crap. The doctor took a good look, did some adjustments, and gave Dad a shot and some more meds. He bandaged him up again and said that he was ready to last another battle. Of course, they all thought that he was going back to the lines to fight. We all played that game, because nobody knew our true plan. I was glad that he was taken care of and I was happy that we were finally treated well. It was nice.

I knew our escape was close, however, because I started to feel a bit of anxiety. I didn't know why but now, looking back, I realize it was the excitement and agony of leaving my country. We were going to a different place completely. Not knowing where or how we would make it. A new language. A new everything. Just the three of us to conquer the world. I won't lie, I was excited as well. Thank goodness for that, because I was quickly reminded that I had to face a terrible enemy again, the nasty Radica. The one that made me feel like a cockroach. I didn't want to feel that way again, but I kept the worry inside. My youth, resilience, and excitement kept me going with a positive attitude.

The day was finally here. It was an early morning, a little chilly, and the sun was just coming out. We gathered our one bag that we had, plus a few snacks and water. I looked at that little cottage for the last time, realizing that was our last home we would have in my country. We left it in the emerging sunlight and walked to the main base, where there was a combi that would take us to the busses. Mom was nervous, but excited. Finally, all she had worked so hard for was coming to fruition. She wanted her family safe and out of this war and doom. She wanted us to live safely.

The beautiful orange glow of the sun was majestic, nature again comforting me. The wind brushed my face as the road took me to the next level. It was weird. Every time I went to the next level, the nature was there, guiding me. There were always signs: from birds, the sun, the little shapes of hearts everywhere in nature. Nature was there to guide me, push me in the right direction, and protect me. It was there to get me where I needed to go. I will never forget the beauty of those mountains. As troubled as they were, they were still my mountains.

As we came to the base, I was scared. The soldiers were everywhere. They looked dirty and mean. They were looking at all of us from head to toe, especially my mom and I. Dad played the role of a higher commander, showing his ID from the other base. It was an ID of honor, so he showed it and firmly demanded the nasty soldiers, "Sit up straight, soldier, and honor your higher officers, before I tear you apart and send you to the muds." Dad looked mean and he played the part well, the soldiers would immediately respond. It was epic. I felt so proud. Those lowlifes deserved it. Inside the base, Mom went to get the tickets. She showed them some papers and the lady behind the counter took one second – then the tickets were in Mom's hands. Not even a word was said.

I still don't know what or how she got those tickets but she did it. Dad, with his chest pumped up, walked right next to her. The soldiers inside saluted him and the ladies smiled at all of us. They all looked as if the teacher had walked in to a room full of rowdy kids. It felt great. The lady showed us the way to the buses, which were waiting to depart in the next twenty minutes. I felt such adrenaline, excitement, and fear all at once. At least I had Dad with me, my protector, and Mom. We were whole again, but still we were going away into the unknown. This was different than any trip I ever took before, different than any bus ride I took before. The fear of the bus stranding us again was there, or soldiers killing us, or so many things going wrong all flashing through my mind.

We walked as fast as we could toward Bus #9. Since we only had one little bag, we sped up. Before we knew it, we were at the front door of the bus. I looked over my shoulder, just in case someone was going to stop us or kill us. The bus driver asking us to show our tickets startled me. Mom gave them to him, "I see no luggage so, welcome aboard." I was shocked, things were going way too smoothly. I was waiting for a disaster. We walked slowly up the stairs of the gray bus. It was a pretty modern bus and it looked comfortable. Once we got in, there were mostly civilians, perhaps some other refugees too, one or two soldiers, and some older ladies too. It was pretty empty, so it was easy to find spots. We sat down, Mom and I together and Dad right next to us by himself.

The bus had a musty smell, mixed with smoke – as everyone always smoked there. It was run down, but still in good shape. It definitely beat the freezer truck. We finally got situated, looking around anxiously a few more times but, to our surprise, the atmosphere was calm. I think all these people just wanted to get out safely. To my surprise, the driver was a nice guy too. I fully expected it to be the one of the nasty soldiers, but it seemed to be another refugee or just a more humble guy. We sat, eager to leave and just absorbed the quiet setting. Everyone was sitting on eggshells, as I liked to say. I looked out of the window. Even in the smog, there was still the beauty of the mountains, and a little cloud that was in the shape of a heart so pronounced that I knew that it was a message that we were going to be okay. The beauty again calmed me down.

No more people came on, and the bus was half full. The driver checked on everyone and said, "We're ready to go. Take your seats. We have a long ride." We were riding to Belgrade, in the heart of Serbia. Another day or so being surrounded by the Serbians. Throughout this chaos, I had learned that hate spreads really fast. It turns people into monsters. I saw mean people, but I also saw that not all people were like that. Some people were good and willing to help. I learned that love is stronger, like the love of our small family.

The beginning of the trip was rough. We had to go through some tunnels and dirt roads. It was loud and scary. I held Mom's hand firmly and Dad was holding us from the back seat, "All will be okay, my little angel." We set our course to Belgrade, but we had to go through barricades first. The soldiers had to stop us and, every time they did, all of our hearts fell down to the floor. We were afraid that we would end up just another casualty in the woods. Just another murder. Dad would kind of hide behind the seat, so that the soldiers would not look or recognize him. The barricades were not that bad after all. They were short. Once they saw that our bus was mostly full of old, unattractive ladies and children, they left quickly. The driver would give them some official papers in an envelope. All I know was that they left quickly when they saw the envelope. I would not doubt that it was bribe money. Dirty money. I am not sure how Mom did it. It looked like all of these other people had higher-end families that paid money to get their loved one out. Our escape was never a sure bet, however. There were psychos everywhere. For many, getting money or getting to rape or kill was the same.

We continued on for an hour or so before we relaxed a bit. Even if we heard shots and falling grenades, I had heard them enough to know that these were miles away. At that point, grenades could certainly hit us. We just had to hope that this trip was legitimate and we would not end up in a concentration camp. As if he could smell my anxiety, Dad whispered to me, "Remember, honey.

You are meant to do something great. So, don't worry. We will survive and be well." He smiled and held me tight. I had goosebumps come over my body and a sense of calmness. I would look up and see the beautiful curves of the mountains and the road that was hugging it. We were there with the massive mountains full of trees, vegetation, rocks, and steep forests. The road was curved and cut just right for cars to go by. The nature was mesmerizing. I felt at peace. I think I got lost in that beauty. I even think that I dosed off for a while, because I know the trip had to be a few hours.

I heard an echo of a falling grenade in the distance. As I looked around, both parents were alert and super close to me. The looks on their faces were a little worrisome. Before I knew it, we were all holding our breath and the tension was so thick that you could have cut it with a knife. Then I realized that we were approaching the main base, Pale, and my heart skipped a beat. I was scared. This was the base where Dad escaped from, the soldiers and commanders are still there. *Will they search the bus and recognize him? Will they take my dad? Will they kill us all?* The questions were flowing out of my head as I turned to Dad and, as if he knew every question I was aching to ask, "Don't worry. We will just pass by. Just another quick checkpoint. Nobody will even get in." I wanted to believe him, but I closed my eyes and sat on top of Dad, just in case they did see him. I held him tight. Mom sat in the seat in front of us.

As we approached, I heard a lot of commotion, mostly from outside. Folk music was playing, there were a few shots fired, I felt Dad holding me harder. Then we stopped, I couldn't help but peek. I saw the camps and many soldiers. In the fields around, there were tanks and big artillery. They stopped the bus, and one of the soldiers signaled the driver to open the door. All our hearts dropped to the floor. You could hear people's stomachs growling, it was so silent. The soldier boarded and said to our driver, "Where are you headed?" The driver answered,

"Belgrade. These are very important family members of our bravest soldiers." The soldier quietly looked around. I didn't move a muscle, and neither did Dad or Mom. Then I heard the driver say, "Here are the transport papers." The soldier sighed and looked through them for a few minutes, before giving them back and asking if there were any weapons on board. The driver assured him not. The soldier stood there, then he took a few more steps inside, asking one of the passengers, "What is your name?" A little squeaky woman's voice responded, "Radacic." A true Serbian name. The solder shuffled through the papers, "Ah! There you are. General Radacic's aunt. That's nice… okay then! You guys take care and tell Belgrade that you have the best soldiers here fighting for our Serbia. We will prevail and take our land back."

A few voices replied "yes" with fearful voices, then the soldier growled in a nasty voice, "Get going! You are holding up my lunch." I heard his steps, walking down the stairs of the bus, and the door closed. I peeked over Dad's shoulder to watch the soldier step out and head to the side to open the barricade. As the bus started driving away, we passed the barricade and headed down the road. The second we did that, all of the passengers just exhaled and relaxed. We all started smiling and feeling the relief. I got into my own seat and hugged Mom, just after I kissed Dad and hugged him too. I noticed we were all sweating profusely, but it was over. We passed the worst part. I looked at Mom, "How did you pull this off? Those papers?" She responded, "Don't even ask. It was tough, but so am I. And you know what? So are you, my love."

The passengers got comfortable and started talking amongst themselves. Before we knew it, we were on a regular highway, off the dirt road from the base camp. We saw a few military cars heading to Pale from Serbia, and that's when we knew that we were a little safer. We had just crossed the Serbian border. We were all exhausted and truly emotionally drained, but we knew that, from here, it should not get any worse. It could just be a new beginning for us. I lay on Mom's lap and, as she caressed me, I went to sleep. I swear I dreamt that we were going to Turkey or Dubrovnik for vacation. I had a nice nap and I felt relaxed, finally. I dreamt of blue water, a nice pool, and just so much fun and relaxation. I will never forget that dream. I would drift on and off as the road hit a bump or two and, once I woke up for sure, I got up to see the outskirts of the city of Belgrade.

Chapter Twenty-Nine

I felt relieved about being close to Belgrade, but also anxious. I just took it as is, happy to be away from grenades and death. In the city, we headed to Belgrade's main bus stop. We drove in slowly, as the traffic got heavier. As night fell, the lights illuminated the city. Again, it was strange to see how, in this part of the country, it didn't seem like we were in this brutal civil war at all. It looked like these people went on with their lives as if nothing was happening. There were no ruins, no turmoil, everything was normal.

We finally came to the station. There were a few people there, waiting for the passengers who leaned toward windows on one side to see their loved ones. Vania, Radica's mom, was picking us up. My anxiety was kicking in, because I didn't want to go through that turmoil again. This time, however, it was only going to be for a day or so. We parked and got off the bus. Mom pulled me to the side, "Don't worry. Nothing will hurt you anymore. We are only here for a day." I took her hand and followed and we found Vania. She greeted us so nicely, with a huge hug and smile. She gave Dad preferential treatment. Again, he was viewed as a war hero and a Serbian soldier. I wanted to tell them that he would never become a Serbian soldier, but we took the friendly treatment, and used it to the max.

We rode straight to the house, the last house we'd be in before we left this country by plane. Mom used Dad's lie to have Vania help us out. Vania asked questions and talked to my parents. I tuned her out and just watched out of the window of the car. They were talking about the war and how we survived. Mom and Dad kept it very vague and somewhat filled with lies, all in order not to get found out. After all, we were staying in enemy lands here. My mom even spoke about the glory of Serbians and how she was wrong before. She kept confirming how the Serbian legacy was correct. This was obviously impossible, as Bosnia was so intermixed. All the war was achieving was death and generations deleted. They believed in that violence, however, and it was toxic. I focused on the lights and enjoyed the normalcy for a bit. We finally came to the house. My stomach was turning. I didn't want to encounter the grandma and didn't want to be afraid to go through their bedroom. I was more scared of the mental abuse here than the actual war and death by grenade. At least bullets were honest and blunt and quick. Mental abuse is sneaky and much scarier.

To my surprise, they had taken the grandparents to the house next door, so they could leave us the little house to ourselves. How wonderful! We had some privacy. Vania said, "I know you must be tired, so we will have breakfast for you tomorrow. Get some rest. We love you." I knew she loved my Mom, and she was a great friend to help, but she definitely had much more love for this false version of my Dad, "the Serbian war hero" in her house. I do have to say that regardless of everything we were and always will be very thankful for their help. We took it and went with it. We used the bathroom to wash off. Finally, a real shower again. We put away the one bag of luggage we had and went to bed. My parents used the bed where the grandparents usually slept and I went in to the bed Mom and I had shared before. I didn't want to close the door between my parents and me. I was scared. It was strange to be alone. It was unfamiliar, but my parents kissed me good night and told me everything would be okay. We were safe now. As they went to their bed, I laid there in darkness. I listened to the silence and again could not fall asleep. I was missing the sound of grenades, even the distant echoes of bullets I heard in the mountains. The anxiety of unfamiliar was taking over me. I closed my eyes and imagined our old house.

When I woke, my parents were talking to the grandparents. They were praising Dad, bringing him fruit and bread, water and cognac, admiring his wounded leg. The grandpa hugged Dad and just rejoiced over him. I watched and laughed inside. Dad saw me and gave me a look: *Don't you dare say anything*. He smirked and told me to come give him a hug. I came out and said hello to everyone and hugged Dad, "I'm enjoying this too. You are my hero." Vania, Nenad and Radica came in a little later. My stomach dropped seeing her but again, to my surprise, she was super nice. She hugged me and talked to me, being respectful. I'm not sure if it was fake or not, but I did not mind. I was relieved. The day was actually pleasant, but I'm glad it was not too long, as we needed to get going to the airport.

Chapter Thirty

I still didn't believe it. We were going to Spain. *Wow, what's in Spain? How can we do this? How can we live? How are we going to fit in? We have nothing with us! Just our tiny bag. We have no money. We don't even know Spanish!* It just hit me: *What in the world are we going to do!?!* My anxiety was rising again. I did not know what to think, but it took my focus off the time with Radica. We ate a great home-cooked meal – pitas, little sausages, and lots of bread and chocolate. I was in heaven. I hadn't eaten like that in a while. The conversation had been going on for a while, I would tune in and out and couldn't really get my head around how I was about to go to another country completely. How I was moving on from fearing death in a basement to brave adventure in a different world. It was like we were parachuting into a different world to start a new life. *Who was I? What was I meant to do?*

The adults would get louder at times and that would jerk me back to the present moment. They would talk about old times, which was nice. The beautiful peace that used to exist when a Muslim woman and a Serbian woman could be best friends. That was the time when we lived together in peace and love and now; I was forever leaving my country, my family, and my heritage. I was sad and heartbroken about just that part. I was leaving all of my family and everything we had. I was scared, nervous, and unstable but, when you have no choice but to move forward, you just go.

We finished up our meal and Dad finished telling them his stories. Before I knew it, we needed to get ready to go to the Belgrade airport. So, we started to say our goodbyes. I remember the grandpa never wanting to let go of my dad, hugging him and showing appreciation. It was funny, Vania hugging Mom and

Radica giving me a fake half-hug. I said my goodbyes with my focus on our next chapter. We got into a car and were on our way to the airport. I again observed the lights and calmness. We were coming to one of my most favorite places. I love airports. There is something about the freedom of an airplane. I had travelled all my life, so it didn't faze me. It fascinated me.

We were dropped off at the entrance by Nenad, as it was not too far from the house. We walked to the counter, and Mom went first to give them the tickets. They checked us all in. Of course, we didn't have any luggage. Just our bag. It was heartbreaking that, after all we used to have – houses, cars, all our possessions – the only thing we were leaving with was that little bag with nothing in it. All our lives erased and summed up in one bag and lots of memories and experience. As the lady was checking us in, she asked for a few papers and permission slips and passports. Mom had it all.

I couldn't believe it. I was going into another country – and it was not for vacation. It was for life. How difficult would it be to be refugees in a different country if being a refugee here was pure hell? My mind was racing. Dad and Mom held me tight as we walked through the airport. We walked slowly and diligently, watching who was around. We were scared that we would be discriminated against, or that Dad would be recognized, transported back, or plainly just killed. To my surprise, however, everything felt perfectly normal. There were a few military personnel. There were security checks that we went through with flying colors. One guy called us diplomats. We were in a war-tormented airport, but it still functioned normally. The people in it couldn't have cared less who we were and where we were going. It was strangely peaceful.

We found our gate and sat there with the other passengers and military personnel. It was not long before we boarded a double decker transatlantic plane. It was pretty full, and we were packed in the center of the middle section like sardines. I still couldn't believe we were boarding the plane and we were united. At that time, smoking was allowed in certain areas of planes, so the inside still smelled like smoke. It looked like the whole plane was filled with refugees trying to escape to find a new life. The pilot came on the speaker, "Our destination is Barcelona."

The stewardesses went by to check on all of us and they were very nice. I remembered why I always wanted to be a stewardess. They were pretty and nice and travelled around the world. We were all getting ready for the engines to start for takeoff. Just as I asked Mom if we were leaving soon, the plane started moving forward. We looked to the left, because there were not too many people in those seats, and we could see through the window.

We saw the airport and, slowly as we ascended, we saw mountains, cities and more detail. As always, I got butterflies in my stomach as we took off, just like I used to get when we travelled. However, even if that feeling was back, it was so different this time. As we took off, I saw the beautiful mountains, the city, the entire country. I saw the smoke and ruins and destruction as ugly scars on a beautiful child. I saw my country dying of cancer, and that view will always be engraved in my heart.

That will be my scar for the rest of my life. The nature is still there, my nature that nurtured me for so long. It is still there, but it is sad. The mountains are beautiful, but they are sad. That view looked like my country was crying, as I cried with it. My country, my home, and my previous life were all there. This was not a vacation trip. This was real life. Watching my home disappear in clouds, while shedding tears. Mom held my hand and I saw Dad speechless. They were both teary-eyed and breathing heavy. My tears went down my cheeks as Mom wiped them, "We will be okay. We will come back one day." I looked at her with the fear of a brave but unknown future ahead of me. Ahead of all of us, "How are we going to survive? How will we live in a foreign country? We don't even speak Spanish?" She simply replied, "We will. Very well. Like we always do. It will be a fun, a new adventure."

She gave me hope then, and my persona was marked right then and there as an adventurer as a survivor. I continued looking at the clouds and my country disappearing slowly, as part of my soul and heart was left behind. All we had with us were memories. What was in store for us now? We had nothing and no one in a strange country. With my mother and father beside me, however, I knew that we were strong enough to conquer anything. My name is Manja, and I am a War survivor.

Made in the USA
Middletown, DE
17 September 2019